WARRIOR FORGOTTEN

A Native American's Perspective of Vietnam

GENE CULLY

For special discounts on bulk purchases,
please email Sales@KastPublishing.com.

ISBN: 978-0-9962097-3-1
Printed in the United States of America.

WARRIOR FORGOTTEN

A Native American's Perspective of Vietnam

KAST PUBLISHING, LLC

Acknowledgements

I would like to thank my friends from Golf Company Second Battalion, Fourth Marines for their support and for everything they've done on my behalf. They witnessed the same horrible events and, like me, they will never forget the pain and sorrow of that day. These courageous men who fought in Vietnam gave it their all and will never be forgotten in my mind and heart.

I would also like to thank Laine Cunningham, Consultant, Writers' Resource, Inc., for her assistance with reading my manuscript and editing, where needed. And to Sherry Kast of Kast Publishing, LLC, thank you for your willingness to work with me to publish "Warrior Forgotten" so I could leave a legacy for my family.

Finally, I would like to give a special thanks to my wife, Maribeth. She always believes in me and encourages me to do what is best. She provided unlimited support in my quest to write this book. Without her encouragement, I never would have finished this story.

Introduction

I wrote this book after a discussion with another Golf Company survivor of a firefight in Vietnam on September 21, 1967. We were discussing the "lost medal" for which I had allegedly been recommended. He encouraged me to put my thoughts down on paper and hopefully get some exposure about the firefight and the courageous men we fought alongside with that day.

He notified another survivor from that horrific day, and that man eventually contacted me through email. He thought I'd been killed because the last time he'd seen me, I was standing out in the open returning cover fire and getting wounded Marines off the battlefield. He said our platoon sergeant had indeed recommended me for the Navy Cross for my actions that day.

After all these years, I've wondered about the missing documents concerning the recommendation and elusive medal.

Later in life as I traveled throughout the United States as an artist, I talked with other Native American Indian veterans about the Vietnam War. Their experiences further prompted me to write this book. They gave me hope and assured me that things eventually come full circle in life.

Writing this book gave me the opportunity to set the record straight about my actions. It has also helped me to stop second-guessing the events. I took great pride in helping my fellow Marines during the firefight. We all had a job to do. We knew what we had to do to survive. We also knew that, even though other Marines didn't make it, our actions were not in vain.

Although I was more than willing to tackle this writing task, the details of the ordeal were difficult to face. As the painful memories unfolded, it was a challenge for me to overcome the loss, grief, and mixed emotions I'd endured during the firefight and for more than forty years thereafter.

As I worked during the last few years to face these difficult emotions, I sought help from the former commander of Second Battalion, Fourth Marines. He'd been the senior officer during the September 1967 incident. He took my information with the hope of forwarding a recommendation for the Navy Cross and/or other medal for which I may have been recommended, but unfortunately he has passed away.

In December 2006, I sent an inquiry letter to a Texas senator, but received no response. A couple of other survivors from the September '67 firefight tried to assist by contacting a senator in Pennsylvania when I lived up north. The issue is still pending.

While waiting, I finished writing this book. Stories from my childhood and school years are presented to help readers understand my background and how I got to Vietnam. I am a Native American Indian and I want readers to know about the culture and heritage of my people. I also want readers to know how my culture, as well as the excellent training provided by the Marine Corps, helped me during my tour of duty. Finally, I want the men I fought with to be seen as brave and valiant.

During the past few years, I've recalled stories from my upbringing and my family's struggles to survive. These memories stirred up mixed emotions. I'm grateful to have had such wonderful parents. I had nothing as a child but love. Being without so many of life's material things made me a survivor. This instinct served me well in Vietnam, coupled with my military training and pride in serving my country. I was both a Marine and a survivor.

This book is both humorous and emotional. Except for the actual names of my friends, I have provided as much detail as possible of the events, when they took place, and how they occurred. I tried to reveal what happened without being hurt emotionally and without input from other survivors. I have recorded it here as best I could.

When I thought about everything that happened during that one firefight in September, my hands and knees shook and trembled. As I wrote that chapter, my right foot tapped the floor and my left hand drummed the underside of my chair. My throat ached with frustration and sadness for the loss of my friends.

Even when I returned to the present, the jittery feelings stuck with me. When I reached for my coffee, I realized it had gotten cold. I had been caught up in vividly remembering the loss of the brave and courageous Marines still in the field after I left. I wondered if I was going to be able to sleep that night.

Now here's my story. I hope you enjoy it and are inspired by the courageous, loyal, and dedicated men who sacrificed their lives so others could survive.

– Gene Cully

An Eyewitness Account
A letter from Tim Frederick to Gene Cully, April 2005

On the morning of September 21, 1967, I was assigned as a machine gun squad leader with the 1st Platoon Golf Company 2nd Battalion, 4th Marine Regiment. That morning, like many other mornings, I was not given much information as to the why and where of what we were to do. All that I remember is that we were to go out in support of other units, search for the enemy, and destroy them if found. Not much different than any other day. My account of the events is what I witnessed, and remember. I've learned over the years that eyewitness accounts of events can be quite different from eyewitness to eyewitness. One person sees something and another, looking at the same thing, can see it differently.

The day started out beautiful sun shine hot humid, not unlike a day in Louisiana, where I'm from. I was walking along with my friend who was also from Louisiana. As I remember, we were on line sweeping through an open area with a tree line in front of us and a dry ditch or creek bed over to my right....shortly, this beautiful day would become the worst of the worst days. The terror the horror that is war would come down on me and my friends in Golf Company. It was late in my tour. I was a "short timer" at the time, but everything I had done and everything I had seen up to this time would pale in comparison. The proud history of the Second Battalion, Fourth Marine Regiment would get a new chapter that day. Some of my friends would write it with their blood some with their lives everyone would add something.

I don't know who hit us or what hit us. I just knew they did. All of a sudden the mortar rounds started coming in, machine gun fire and small arms fire from everywhere!! I remember looking up at one point and seeing the mortar rounds falling like rain drops, they were that thick. Things started to explode, people started to explode, the noise was deafening. My friend ... was calling my name right next to me. I could hardly hear him. He was on his back and said he'd been hit. I crawled over to him. He said he was hit in the back and leg. I rolled him over and saw that the back of his leg from his hips down was gone! I only had one small bandage that we carried. It was useless on a wound of that size, useless! The explosions kept coming. Calling for a corpsman was useless. The noise, the chaos, no one could hear!!! I wrapped my small bandage around his leg as tight as I could. I told him he would be all right. I told him I would go for help and would return. I never saw him again. Later, in the rear, I learned that he had died of his wounds.

I tried to find my gun team. They were walking not far ahead of me when the shooting started, I could not find them in the confusion. There were small groups here and there behind any cover that we could find, returning fire at an unseen enemy, and mortar rounds kept coming! Everyone not dead or wounded was trying to locate the enemy, someone, I don't know who was trying to get everyone to a dry ditch for cover. While trying to get there I came upon the body of … a good friend who had joined the 2/4 the same time I had. I stayed with him for a while, and then continued to try to make it to the ditch….then it seemed like the mortar rounds zeroed on the ditch. Couldn't move. After some time I was able to move along the ditch and that's when I came up on another friend … sitting there, dazed look on his face. I saw that he had taken a hit to his lower leg. What was there was just hanging on by the tendons. He was calm he didn't seem to be bleeding much, I didn't have any bandages and neither did he. We talked, I noticed an unexploded mortar round just feet from him. If that had gone off he would be dead … I told him I would get help and return. I never saw him again.

I made it further up the ditch where we could return fire into the tree line. The enemy was still unseen. There was an open area to my left and I heard yelling from that direction and looked out across there and saw Corporal Gene Cully standing firing and on the ground next to him was one of our corpsman … appeared to be wounded and Corporal Cully was providing cover fire, standing in the open! Gene is yelling, firing, but calm just standing there. I and the Marine next to me decided to go get corpsman … while Gene is covering. We make it to him, he is shot in the stomach, bullets whizzing everywhere, by this time Gene has reloaded or gotten another rifle off the ground or something, but he's standing firing again, the incoming on us stop and we are able to get [the corpsman] behind some cover. Corporal Cully is still standing firing...I thought to myself, He'll be dead soon!!! Corporal Cully standing firing is the last time I saw him.

Time was stopped. I can't tell you how long this insanity lasted, this never ending firing being fired at finding friends bodies, finding others wounded, telling them I'd be back only to never see them again. I remember finding a hole and just sitting there. I had had enough I quit...someone came and sat next to me and said it was over, we were heading out, after a while I got out of the hole. We had to carry wounded and dead back to a place we had left so long ago that day. We carried some dead back, but later I learned that we had left 18 bodies out on the battlefield. How could this be? Who made that decision? Marines never leave their dead, right? But we had ... the dead were recovered 19 days after the battle, there was talk that one was actually taken prisoner, that was never confirmed during my tour, at least not to me, like I said earlier I wasn't too high on the need to know chain.

Every time I go back to that battlefield, and I do go back often, I am amazed at what I witnessed and survived, so much courage. So much disregard for personal safety. Brave men. I am honored and humbled to have been in the presence of such men.

Eyewitness...I saw one thing. What did Corporal Gene Cully see? I saw one of the bravest acts I'd seen during my tour. He on the other hand saw three of the most frightened people he may have ever seen....In the rear later, Sgt. Nelson, our platoon Sgt. told me that Cully had been put in for a Navy Cross. I told him that if anyone ever deserved it Corporal Gene Cully did...never heard anymore no one ever asked me any details of that day until now...Being an unreliable, but alive, eyewitness to Corporal Cully's bravery, and total disregard of his own personal safety while knowingly or unknowingly saving the lives of two Marines and one much loved Navy Corpsman, what can I say, I saw what I saw.....It is good to go back and be 20 again!!!!

Chapter One

The Warrior

If I have done any deed worthy of remembrance, that deed will be my monument, if not, no monument can preserve my memory.
Agesilaus II, King of Sparta (circa 444-360 B.C.)

I was twenty years old when I first shot someone.

Snipers were part of the guerrilla warfare and terror tactics the Viet Cong (VC) used. They hid in tall trees and heavy jungle cover. They targeted American and South Vietnamese Army officers as a way to disrupt command. They slowed military movement and distracted troops while their own fled or closed in. The threat of attack was constant.

During one of our patrols toward the western mountain range, a platoon in our company made a quick sweep through a small village. Suddenly the platoon came under sniper fire. Usually the enemy would stay hidden and continue sporadic fire or sneak off. This time, a sniper ran out from his original position and hid behind some small brush.

He was still well hidden from the platoon that had taken the fire. The undergrowth was so thick in many parts of the bush that we rarely saw the enemy. Bamboo grew in close thickets and vines hung down in the forests. Even the deltas were thick with shrubs and fruit trees used by the civilians for food.

That day, though, First Platoon was in luck. As we came over a small hill, we spotted the sniper. We were behind him and caught him off guard. The entire platoon opened fire. It was over in seconds.

My training with the Marines, both in boot camp and before shipping out, had been intense. I'd already served nearly a year of active duty before going overseas. Everything had prepared me for combat, to act under pressure and to help my fellow troops. But, nothing had prepared me for the first time I would see a man I helped kill.

As I looked at the sniper lying on the ground, I felt bad. He was VC. He was flesh and blood just like me, but he was the enemy. I thought about the many other snipers who killed my Marine brothers and gotten away. This was war. I had a job to do. I did my job and would keep doing it until ordered to stand down.

As we moved on, I tried not to think about whether my bullet had dealt the killing wound to this particular sniper. We'd all opened up on him at the same time. Since I'd been rated a sharpshooter on the rifle range, it was unlikely that I'd missed him entirely. But seeing the enemy out in the open, seeing that he was a man and then for the first time watching someone die, isn't something any Marine forgets.

Several days later we came down from the mountain. Either the VC or a villager had buried the sniper at the same location.

* * *

I am from the Raccoon Clan with the Te' Wah' le Band of the Seminole Nation. I was born October 17, 1945, in a small town called Konawa in the southeastern part of Oklahoma. Konawa is about sixty-five miles from Oklahoma City, in Seminole County.

My father was Seminole and my mother was Creek. Seminoles are part of the Muskogee peoples, a collection of Florida tribes that gathered together during the Spanish and English border wars, beginning in 1816.

The Great Seminole War was later fought and resulted from the U.S. government's forced attempt to remove the Seminoles from Florida under Payne's Landing Treaty in 1832, a paper that stole our original territory. The war made our tribe's portion of the Indian Removal from the southeast one of the worst. After seven years of fighting and thousands of lost lives, a military escort led most of our people to Oklahoma. The two-month journey in the summer of 1836 resulted in many more deaths.

Seminole means people who left and is from the Creek word, semino le.

My grandparents worked their farm in Seminole County and passed on their knowledge to the next generation. My Dad was a quiet man, the fourth of five children. He was raised working with cattle and horses, as well as tending pigs and chickens. He did a little blacksmithing early in life and had a knack for repairing things.

He was a short man with a stocky build, big bones, and wavy black hair. He was a hard-working man who never complained. He didn't have much of an education...might as well say no education. The story was that he dropped out of second grade to help his ailing mother.

He did general labor work for anyone who was hiring; he was always in demand because of his initiative. He covered just about every skill you'd expect to see in rural areas. He mended fence lines and dug postholes the old fashion way with a posthole digger and a lot of sweat. He also helped farmers and ranchers take their cattle to the sale barn for auction.

Sometimes, I woke in the middle of night to see him finally coming in after a long day of work. He would grab whatever Mom set out for him to eat, clean up, and go right to bed for a short night's sleep.

Early the next morning, he was up and ready to work again. In the kitchen, the wood-burning stove would already be going full blast. Mom always got up before him to make hot biscuits from scratch. A few potatoes were cut up, fried in the skillet, and served with some homemade gravy on the side. Hot water stood ready for Dad's instant coffee. After eating, he waited in front of the house in the early morning darkness for his ride.

He tried to give us the necessities and keep food on the table. He would have given the shirt off his back to help anyone in need without ever expecting anything in return. He spoke very, very little English but was an excellent provider for Mom and the family.

My mother was a full-blood Creek and the youngest of three children. I remember her as a lovely woman, standing 5'1" and weighing about 140 pounds. I don't remember her wearing makeup except a dash of lipstick or a little rouge on her cheeks. She wore her hair in a bun and always had a comb stuck in her bun to keep it in place.

Mom was born deaf. Although she could neither hear nor speak, she made certain sounds to get her message across. She also used sign language, which all of us children learned. We all received a tremendous amount of love and compassion from her. She also gave us strength when we needed it.

To learn to live with her disabilities, Mom attended the Oklahoma School for the Deaf in Sulphur, Oklahoma. She dropped out after only five years. Even though her education was limited, she had excellent penmanship and was a talented artist. Maybe that's where I got my artistic talent.

Mom often showed us kids off to friends and people she'd just met. She made sure we were polite, kept us neat and tidy, and ensured our clothes were always clean. Every day she swept the floor, sewed or mended clothes, washed clothes, and prepared meals which frequently consisted of a pot of beans. Like all mothers, she was a wonderful cook. We struggled at times but at least we didn't go hungry.

I was the fifth of seven children. While growing up, everyone thought I was cute. I was slim, had very black, thick hair, dark eyes, and had a dark complexion. People said I had a mischievous look in my eye, too. My Native American Indian name is Chibon. The elders called me that, and in my native Creek language it translates to "boy." My brothers and sisters called me Sonny.

We never had a lot but we made do. We were grateful for the things we received and we made it through every year by sticking together and working hard. My parents' main goal was to give their children a place to live, a chance at a good education, and three healthy, hot meals daily. The things they taught me while I was growing up played an important role in helping me get through every day in Vietnam.

* * *

The Marine Corp is the smallest of all U.S. military branches, and the most unique. Officially part of the Naval infantry/combined-arms forces, their boot camp is the longest and toughest program of all the services. The training, operations, and philosophy are all geared toward one goal: going into action outside America's boundaries.

In Vietnam, the role was to perform search and destroy missions to locate the enemy and take them out. Some units were assigned to base camps, especially in the northern areas where the enemy troops were more concentrated. Even then, though, search and destroy patrols were part of the mission.

When U.S. Marines first entered Vietnam, one of their tasks was to defend the Da Nang Airfield, a combat base for air supplies and artillery. In April 1965 they set up an additional base at Phu Bai. Soon the restrictions against engaging the enemy were lifted and Marines began reconnaissance operations. By July 1966, the Demilitarized Zone (DMZ) saw heavy fighting. Additional bases were set up at Dong Ha, Cam Lo, Gio Linh, and the Rockpile.

Since the Marines were such a specialized group, they were outfitted with fewer artillery pieces than Army units. The Navy helped shore up our firepower by supporting Marines in the field. Whenever fighting occurred near the coast, naval gunships that were within range provided fire support.

Although Marine and Army tactics began to merge in the latter half of 1968, the services supported each other whenever possible but operated independently. Many factors made the Vietnam War the deadliest conflict Marines had ever seen. The casualties suffered by the troops exceeded the total count for World War II.

Chapter Two
Okinawa

"Every man has to seek in his own way to make his own self
more noble and to realize his own true worth."
Albert Schweitzer (date unknown)

I was shipping out to Vietnam. The men I trained with boarded buses to the El Toro Marine Corps Air Station (MCAS) in California. After a one-night lay over, we were up at zero dark thirty taking showers and getting dressed; we made it over to the mess hall for our last breakfast in the States before flying to Okinawa, Japan. We were put on a commercial carrier called the Flying Tiger.

Once we boarded, I tried to get as comfortable as possible. The flight attendants were pretty and I'd have plenty of time to look at them during our time in the air. Although the attendants passed out magazines, playing cards, pillows, and blankets, the flight was pretty boring. After an eight to ten hour flight, we had a short stop in Anchorage, Alaska.

Okinawa would be the second stop on our journey to The Republic of Vietnam. I told my parents I was only going to Okinawa. It would have been difficult to explain things to them about Vietnam. They knew Japan used to be an enemy of the United States, and they were afraid. Mom was especially afraid for my safety so I didn't mention Vietnam.

* * *

I thought about joining the military a couple of times before I actually signed up. When I finally did, everything moved at lightning speed. I was living with my brother in Oklahoma City and worked at the same manufacturing plant with him. While the recruiter took care of the paperwork, I walked back to my brother's house. I can't remember if I was excited or in a state of shock.

My brother had come home from work early and said the foreman was wondering where I was. When I told him what I did, he just laughed. He gave me a bear hug and said, "You son of gun! Good luck, Sonny."

That was around 3:00 in the afternoon. I said to him and my sister-in-law, "See you guys later."

When I walked out, I didn't want to look back. I thought, "This is it, my chance to get away from Oklahoma."

I didn't know for sure when I would leave for boot camp but they shipped me out that night.

A gunnery sergeant was waiting for me. "Everything checked out," he said. "You're good to go. When do you want to leave?"

"As soon as possible."

"As in today?" he asked. "Are you in trouble with the authorities?"

"No," I replied. "I just want to get out of Oklahoma."

"Because you're in trouble?"

"I want to find a skill I can use when I get out," I said.

"OK," he shrugged.

He walked me to the medical section. The room was filled with other young men being inducted. I believe they were draftees. The

8

examination only took about fifteen minutes, so the recruiter took me to yet another office to be sworn in. This room was also packed with inductees. A Marine Corps officer swore us in. Enlisting was over almost before it started.

The gunnery sergeant said, "I am going to put you in charge of the group that's going to the Marine Corps Recruit Depot (MCRD) in San Diego."

He handed me two large packages of orange envelopes.

"These are enlistment documents. Give them to the liaison officer when you arrive at the San Diego airport. If he's not there, give them to the DI."

And that was it. Eight hours after signing up, I boarded the bus that would take me to the MCRD. I was officially on my way to becoming a Marine.

* * *

It seemed like I just put my head down when the pilot's voice said we'd be landing shortly in Alaska. We disembarked but had nothing to do but walk around and window shop. The airport prices were outrageous. I ordered a small cup of coffee and when the cashier said, "Three bucks," I almost said forget it. It was too late, though. She'd already poured my coffee and put it in front of me.

A big commotion in the lobby distracted me from the pricey drink. Everyone with a camera was taking pictures of a huge white polar bear inside a glass case. The bear had been mounted in a standing position and was at least ten feet tall. I'd never seen anything that huge in my life. Nobody would have a chance of surviving an attack by that creature.

After our plane had been serviced, we would board again. I finished every drop of my three-dollar coffee and settled in. The flight to Okinawa would take sixteen hours. As we got airborne, I glanced out the window and saw the ground covered in snow. Maybe it was that strong coffee but I couldn't get comfortable enough to go back to sleep.

My mind drifted back to the important people in my life, family and close friends I met throughout the years. I thought about the things I did before joining the Marine Corps. I thought about partying with my brother and friends. More importantly, I thought about my parents and other family members who helped with all the huge potlucks they held in my honor when I was home on leave.

One particular dinner and prayer service hosted by my aunt kept coming back to me. We played volleyball and basketball all day that particular day. Before dinner, I got cleaned up and waited for my uncle to say grace. Several hours later, the ladies put the food away and washed the dishes while the men set up chairs in the front room.

I was seated in the center of the room at the front. The prayer service was great to listen to, especially in our native language. The sermon lasted about half an hour. Then they stood me up as the family members sang our native songs. The lyrics were all very emotional. I had a hard time fighting back the tears; they streamed down my cheeks as I listened to the words.

I thought about the days when my parents would take us to the Big Meeting at our church. In our culture, the Big Meeting was the last supper of Christ with wine drinking during the evening service. Even though Mom couldn't hear the sermons or the songs, she could still feel the holiness of Christ. We could all feel the holiness.

A camp was set up before the service. The camp houses were owned by different congregants and stood all around the white country church. Services were conducted every night beginning on Wednesday. After each service ended, sandwiches and pastries with coffee, iced tea, and fruit punch or Kool-Aid were served.

In the custom of all native churchgoers, different groups had specific seating arrangements in church. The women sat on the right in three distinct sections. Several benches were placed near the door for guests or backsliders. Toward the middle, more benches facing the center were for the Christian women. Right next to the ministers were seats for the seniors, our elders. The left side was set up the same way for men. Behind the pulpit was a smaller bench for the minister and guest speakers.

The Big Meeting was totally different. The service began around 11:00 a.m. The deacon rang the bell so camp members and guests could get ready. While some people attended the services, others prepared hot food. When the services were almost finished, the bell rang again so any last minute preparations could be made for the noon meal. Once the benediction was complete, the deacon rang the bell a little longer.

The meals were served family style. The women waited on everyone to make sure they enjoyed the food. Seating was similar to the church house with ladies on one side and men on the other. When every seat was occupied, grace was said and the meal was blessed. A man or a woman could bless the meal.

At the dinner and prayer service my aunt hosted, guests and family shook my hand and whispered their blessings to me. Once the sermon and last prayer were over, we adjourned for the evening. Everyone wished me well and God's speed. I thanked my aunt; she was quite the Christian lady. The day made me feel good about my native culture and heritage. I wondered if I would return to more of those dinners.

11

* * *

I must have daydreamed all the way to Okinawa because suddenly the pilot announced that we would be landing at Kadena Air Base. The aircraft circled the island. Looking out the window, I spotted lots of fishing boats in the water. As the plane came in low, we could see people moving about in their yards and rice paddies. The traffic looked like it was moving very slowly along the twisted, narrow highways.

It was a hot eighty-six degrees when we landed. The heat poured into the aircraft before I even got to the door. As I stepped outside, the humidity hit me. Our duffle bags were stacked along the tarmac. A group of Marines loaded the bags into a canvas-topped truck. We boarded some buses and headed up the highway to Camp Hansen.

The country was so different than the States. The streets were narrow and a few tiny cars pushed through the villages we passed. I never imagined I'd ever be in a place like that. As we rode along staring at the sights, I wondered when I would see American girls again. The thought of not seeing American girls for the whole thirteen months of my tour was pretty scary.

A town called Honoko sat just outside Camp Hansen. Some of the Marines said they were going out that night and since they'd been there before, they knew where to go. I didn't want to jeopardize my welfare or health in Okinawa, though, and decided to stay in.

At the barracks, a young sergeant told us what to do with our belongings and what we were supposed to take to Vietnam. We marked our bags with strips of large white tape. The date of rotation was written on the strips along with our names. That was pretty much all we did on the first day, other than starting malaria tablets. A corpsman said to make sure we took them when we arrived in Vietnam.

We had liberty for the rest of the day. I was getting hungry so I went over to the PX, the base store, to grab a snack. The next morning, we were scheduled for another round of shots. This time we'd get the dreaded gamma globulin or GG shot, which was given in our rear ends. It wouldn't have been so bad, except the word was that the needle was more than four inches long.

As I waited my turn, I watched the corpsmen poke different Marines. The troops dropped their trousers and bent over to get the shot. Every time, the corpsman fooled around at a table then turned and slapped their butts. The Marines jumped up yelling, "Oh!"

"I haven't done anything yet," the corpsmen would laugh before slapping the Marine again. Finally he'd inject the needle. I couldn't stop laughing, but when it was my turn, I jumped just as high as the other guys.

We were sore in several places when it was over but we were ready to go to Vietnam.

* * *

Morning finally came. All of us were up early. I stripped my bed and turned in my linens. I took a shower, went to chow, and we cleaned up the barracks. Then we sat around waiting for transportation to Kadena Air Base. While we boarded the Flying Tiger, I took a good look around. "See you in about twelve months," I said.

I sat at the rear of the aircraft. The flight would take about twelve hours. I was hoping someone would call out my name and tell me I didn't have to go, that there had been a mix-up and I was supposed to stay in Okinawa. No such luck. The door closed.

The plane gently lifted off. I looked out the window as we banked over the waters of Okinawa and headed toward South Vietnam. I wondered if the people there would look like the Japanese and if the country would look like Okinawa. So many thoughts were running through my mind.

Chapter Three
Vietnam Bound

Youth is a blunder; manhood a struggle; old age a regret.
Benjamin Disraeli, British Statesman (1804-1881)

The flight to South Vietnam was very, very quiet. Everyone stayed to themselves and didn't want to talk. I don't know if their last night of partying had tired them out or if they were thinking about what we were going to face. It seemed like everyone was deep in thought. Many men had this peaceful look about them. Some, like the Marine next to me, were saying prayers.

I sank deeper into my seat and tried to get some shut-eye. No matter what I did, I couldn't get comfortable. I twisted and turned the entire flight. Again, I started thinking. Thinking about my life, what I had accomplished so far and what I wanted next. I worried because I hadn't told my parents I was going to Vietnam. Was it wrong of me not to tell them?

They were wonderful parents and tried their best raising me and my siblings. They did a good job even with the limited things we had. Sometimes I wondered if we were really content with what we had or could we have set a higher standard of living? We never had much but we survived some tough times.

Despite Mom being deaf and Dad not having an education, we did all right. The devotion Dad showed Mom and us kids more than compensated for any material things we lacked. I wondered if we really were poor. We didn't have the same things most people did, but Mom made good use of what we had. We didn't starve, either for food or for love.

I was proud of my parents, but I also wanted my parents to be proud of my accomplishments. That's what kept me moving toward my own dreams. I knew about Mom's needs and what she'd wanted. Dad did his best to give her those things, even if it had meant working two or three jobs. His love for her was that strong.

When Mom wanted to move the family to town in Konawa, Dad made it happen. The new house had hot and cold running water, and most importantly, electricity. We kids could do our homework with plenty of light. A gas cook stove was also a treat. Dad could concentrate on looking for jobs in the evening and didn't have to chop wood late into the night after work like he did for the wood stove we had in the country.

That was luxury living. Mom and Dad made that happen for us kids. Part of the reason was probably because my older sister, who lived in town, needed Mom to babysit. At any rate, living in town was easier on the whole family. We set better standards for ourselves without even knowing it. Dad even bought a thirteen-inch black-and-white television with rabbit ears. We were in "hog heaven."

Around that time, my two younger sisters and I were living at home. My sisters decided not to attend Jones Academy, an Indian boarding school in Oklahoma, anymore which was so far away that they'd have to live in the dorms. Instead they started school in Konawa which was only a few blocks away from our house. Since I was already going to Vamoosa High, I elected to stay there. Vamoosa was a country school about five miles outside of Konawa. The school was an old, single-story brick structure. The gym was on one side and to the right of the school was a long white building for the grade school. Perhaps a hundred students attended the high school. Eventually I was able to move in with my aunt and uncle out in the country so I could be closer to the school.

I remember the horrible times before we moved when we had to walk to town to buy groceries. The heat and humidity were always terrible and the five-mile trip took forever. Cars passed by, not once stopping to offer a ride. It was especially difficult to see Mom struggling in the hot sun.

I couldn't believe we would actually make that trip on foot. Once we were finished at the store, we carried our groceries back home. Dad took the heavier items like sacks of flour and big bags of potatoes. I was about ten years old so I carried the next heaviest items in a burlap sack or a brown paper bag. We stopped periodically to catch our breath.

I can still picture Dad carrying that big sack of flour over his shoulder and a bag of potatoes as sweat ran down his face. His hat was wringing wet and his shirt was drenched. When he stopped and put everything down, his face would be white from the flour sifting out of the bag. We always laughed. He would just take his handkerchief from his back pocket and wipe his face before picking up that flour again.

Those were hard times for us, walking along the highway watching cars drive by. Many had their windows rolled up so we knew they had air conditioning. It made me so mad that no one stopped to help. The heat of the pavement burned through the soles of my shoes. I could only imagine how the scorching pavement felt under Mom's feet, wearing only thin sandals. Mom never complained. I told myself that if I were ever in a car with air conditioning and I passed families like ours, I would stop to help.

During some of our visits to town, Dad treated us to a meal at a small café famous for their greasy hamburgers. The place had air conditioning so we loved to sit in there and cool off. I always ordered a cheeseburger basket with fries that cost fifty cents. That was a lot of money back then, so the meal was a big splurge. I can still smell those greasy hamburgers today.

Dad would order an extra hamburger and wrap it up to go. I could smell that burger all the way home. We couldn't wait for nightfall after our chores were done. Dad would tell Mom to get the hamburger, which still smelled fresh to me. Mom cut the burger into four pieces: one for her, one for me, and the last two for my two sisters. We didn't mind sharing. This was a special treat for all of us.

As we ate, Mom always asked Dad if he was sure he didn't want any. He always said in our native language, "No. Just shut up and eat."

We sat there eating our miniature burgers and talked about what we wanted in life. We'd say things like, "When I grow up, I'm going to live in a great big house like the rich people and have a servant wait on me, have a nice car and not worry about money for gas."

We also said if we had kids they'd never go hungry, just like Mom and Dad had done for us. The biggest thing was that we never wanted to worry about anything. Instead we'd kick back in a huge chair in the living room with a big color television and enjoy life. We dreamed about not chopping wood and not having to carry buckets of water from the well. Last but not least, we would never let the rain and snow make us wet or cold.

As I thought about the old days, a smile crept onto my face. I had already come so far, most importantly by my decision to join the Marine Corps. I learned so much in such a short time. I spent a year on active duty in Bremerton, Washington, providing guard duty. The skills I learned and the experience I gained would benefit me for the rest of my life.

The Marine training was tough and thorough. Every day, we ran around the fence line of MCRD for three miles. I gazed up at the jets while the drill instructor (DI) led us with a running song. We chanted out the cadence to take our minds off being tired. At the obstacle course, we climbed hand-over-hand up ropes dangling from a railroad tie. It looked simple but for some privates it was like hell if they were still trying to get off the ground when others finished.

Our next challenge was to climb over an eight-foot wall and then the tower. Although it looked easy, that tower was tough. We climbed dry nets up one tower then crossed ropes hand-over-hand to the next tower. At the top, the tower offered a good vantage point. We could see the parade deck and across the bay to the Navy's boot camp.

Once the DIs had shaped our bodies and our minds, we moved on to what I considered the good stuff. During the fourth week of boot camp we went to Edison Range for marksmanship training. I thought it would be great because I was good with a rifle. Everyone looked forward to the training. Finally, we got a chance to fire our rifles instead of cleaning them constantly or using them for exercise.

Some of the privates from Tennessee bet the folks from Kentucky they were better shooters. Those from Kentucky bragged about using windage when they hunted back home.

That was Greek to me. I looked down the sights of my .22, found my target, and fired. If I hit it, fine. If I didn't hit it, I adjusted the sights and fired again, plain and simple.

Camp Margarita, the place we stayed while training at Edison Range, sat up on a plateau. The south end held the regimental headquarters with office buildings and the billeting/barracks buildings. There was also an enlisted men's club. In the middle of the camp stood the mess hall, warehouses, a parade deck, the medical building, a staff club, and a parking lot.

The north end of the camp was a battalion area with an office building, a warehouse, the exchange, and more barrack buildings. All of the buildings were gray concrete with windows. The warehouses were sheet metal and most of the area was dirt with a few paved roads.

Our stay was fun, even though we had to perform mess duty for two weeks. This meant we got up at 0300 hours. When we finished with mess, we started the shooting phase. It was a lot more exciting than I thought it would be; it gave me a chance to see how good I really was.

The sitting position they taught us seemed simple until we tried it. We had to sit on the rear part of our cheeks and lean well forward. Our knees and feet had to be at a 45-degree angle with our ankles straight. The rifle butt was held solidly against one shoulder as the right elbow fit inside the right leg. The closer the elbow was to the ground, the steadier the shot.

This position was never used in combat or a firefight. By training in this position and others, we became familiar with fighting from any position. In combat, Marines might be prone, sitting, or standing, depending on the needs of the moment.

Later, the instructor put me in a seated shooting position I would never have come up with myself and it hurt just a little. "The M-14 has a big kick," several people told me. "If you don't hold it right into your shoulder, it can knock you backwards."

I braced myself for the first round. It was a bull's-eye but the kick never came. On qualification day, I ended up firing a sharpshooter.

Prior to shipping out to Vietnam, I was ordered to attend Infantry Training Regiment (ITR) at Camp San Mateo in California. The nearest town, San Clemente, was nestled right by the Pacific Ocean. The training days were long. We did a couple of night exercises on scouting and patrolling. During the day and at night we practiced assault on a fortified position.

Other training was strictly live fire. While doing protective fire at night, it was awesome to watch the red tracer rounds flaring out in every direction. We ran through the infiltration course and did a lot of camouflage training. We learned how to apply camouflage paint to our faces, how to use natural vegetation on our bodies, and how to apply those same techniques to our fighting holes to conceal them from the enemy.

I received the best training the Marines had to offer. I was part of an elite group and would have the support of other Marines in the field. Although I had no idea what I would find in Vietnam, I was as prepared as any Marine could be.

I had plenty of time to think about things during that long plane ride. I lifted my shade and looked out the window of the aircraft, but all I saw was the deep blue water below and the white clouds drifting by.

Sitting in that airplane heading toward a war zone, my life was really just beginning. I was only twenty years old and the thought of dying had never crossed my mind. Even though I was going to Vietnam, death didn't occur to me. I know that sounds ridiculous, but it's the truth. I've always been positive about things and about myself. This attitude probably helped me through the trying days that would come over the next thirteen months. I just had no idea exactly how trying they would be.

Chapter Four
Da Nang to Phu Bai

Conscience is the inner voice that warns us somebody may be looking.
Henry Louise Mencken

It was April 1967. The pilot said we were ninety miles from Vietnam and we would be arriving in Da Nang. Everyone got extremely quiet; the moment of truth was approaching. As the plane banked, I saw the China Seas and Vietnam.

On a map, Vietnam looks like a bamboo pole with rice baskets hanging at either end. It's very narrow in the middle, only thirty miles across, and widens out to ten times that at the north and south. The entire country is about the size of New Mexico. China sits to the north and a mountain range on the west separates it from Laos and Cambodia.

The southern area is mostly flat. The Mekong River splits into nine smaller rivers, creating a wide, swampy delta. Despite all the pockmarks from bombs and artillery explosions, the soil was still so rich the vegetation was overgrown and rice paddies dominated the countryside. It looked like there was only one highway and everyone was on it.

A lot of lush foliage surrounded the Da Nang Air Base. A road circled the perimeter with high barbed wire protecting it. As the Flying Tiger landed, traffic of all sorts buzzed around the base just like back in

California at Camp Pendleton. Just like home, a fence only separated civilians from the installation. Nearly 150,000 Vietnamese lived within mortar range of the airfield.

As I exited the Flying Tiger, the heat hit me hard. Most of Vietnam has a subtropical climate so it was intense and very humid. I arrived just before the start of the monsoon season when the cooler, drier winter was building up to the rains. Cooler, in this case, was still hot. Before long I was drenched in sweat top to bottom; the sweat was running down both legs and made me uncomfortable.

The scenery reminded me of Okinawa, except here the boom of outgoing artillery fire sounded continually in the distance. A green bus met us on the tarmac. The windows were covered with metal screens to prevent grenades from being thrown in by the VC. We had touched down in a war that was fought as much with guerilla tactics as traditional military movements.

The terminal looked like a carnival. People were everywhere. Personnel from every military branch were there, some coming in and some going home. Even though I just arrived, believe me, I already looked forward to the end of my tour. We staged our bags in a transit area and were shown where to eat and sleep. Later that afternoon someone found a club. Just about everyone from my flight headed over to cool off.

I stayed behind and found a cot near the entrance. A sandbagged bunker sat right outside. Periodically the air base was attacked, so I didn't want to take any chances. Fortunately nothing significant happened that night, just a lot of outgoing artillery fire and illumination flares. A siren went off once so we took cover in the bunker. When the all-clear sounded, I fell back onto my cot and had a good night's sleep.

The next day felt like a regular day with personnel moving about, going to the mess hall, making coffee from leftover C rations, and shooting the breeze. A couple of guys said they were going down to China Beach to check things out. I wasn't going anywhere. I was anxious to join my unit. When some of the guys actually headed down to the beach, I changed my mind. I was a little scared about going out to an unknown area but said, "What the heck."

We caught a personnel carrier going that direction. The carriers were nothing more than oversized jeeps converted into small pickups. They could carry seven people, six in the back and one with the driver. It dropped us at China Beach in no time.

The area was mostly a collection of vendors, like an outdoor market set up in a village. Cooking smells filled the air. Mostly I remember the scent of onions. There was a smell of the city that was hard to describe, but once you smelled it, the scent stayed with you.

All along China Beach, villagers were selling everything they could lay there hands on. I saw more American cigarettes being sold there than in the PX back home. The favorites were Salem and Kool, with Winston and Marlboro both a solid second. There were also some Camel and Lucky Strike packets.

The vendors even had hard liquor like Johnny Walker Red and Black, Cutty Sark, Seagram's 7, and Canadian Club. A few beers sat on the shelves in the markets. Carling Black Label, Pabst Blue Ribbon, and of course, Schlitz were available. You name it, they had it. If they didn't have it, I'm sure they could have rounded it up from somewhere.

I wondered where the vendors got all that stuff. It turned out that troops had been on the ground in large numbers for two years. Thousands of U.S. military advisors had arrived years before that to help the South Vietnamese military forces resist the communist forces.

By the time I arrived in South Vietnam, it was inundated with manufactured goods. Its entire economy was transformed.

That day at China Beach not only introduced me to the black market, I also had my first encounter with the Vietnamese people. They were small and wore what looked like black pajama bottoms with white shirts or blouses. The loose fit and lightweight fabric made the outfit very comfortable for that climate. The pant bottoms were also wide enough to be easily rolled up while people worked in the rice paddies.

The Vietnamese people used what they had and did what they needed to for survival, much like my parents. I would have to be resourceful and rely on those same survival skills in the Vietnam jungles and mountains for the next thirteen months of my life.

* * *

It was about 1300 hours when I checked in with the Marine liaison at the manifest area. I was headed to the Third Marine Division I Corps. I didn't know where they were located much less know what I Corps stood for. Apparently the Third Marine Division was in the field a good deal of the time.

The excitement at check in was like Christmas. Everybody was asking, "Where are you going?" and "What division did you get?" After check in, I went to Freedom Hill with a couple other Marines to convert some of my greenbacks over to Military Pay Certificates (MPC).

MPCs were the serviceman's money in Vietnam. Just like the U.S. dollar, the bills had values of $1, $5, $10 and $20. The $20 value was the most common. Each MPC had a different color to designate the value.

They were used at military exchanges and clubs, and could be converted to American currency before leaving Vietnam.

I was so anxious to check in with my outfit that I couldn't sleep. I stayed up late thinking. Reveille came pretty early. After morning chow, we boarded a waiting KC-130 transport plane. The propellers were revved up pretty fast as it sat on the tarmac. It was ready to roll, and so was I.

The plane's interior was as basic as it could get. There were no seatbelts, cushions, or bathroom. A scout dog and his handler sat toward the back near some supplies. I kept my distance in case the dog was mean. I heard about the mess those dogs could leave after a meal. If the dog had an accident, though, it was back where the heavy wind that came through the open cargo door would hopefully circulate the smell away.

The rest of the seats were taken by a mix of Marines. New men like me wore the stateside utility uniform or green dungarees. The majority of the personnel wore jungle fatigues. A few passengers had their dog tags tucked in their boot laces. Some of the Marines were dirty and looked tired. One guy said they had just come back from rest and recreation (R&R).

The KC-130 moved slowly down the runway. The engine was deafening. No one bothered to talk much because no one could hear a word. When we finally lifted off, it seemed like we shot straight up. No one had told us about flying times or emergency procedures yet everyone seem relaxed. We were all headed for I Corps, the Third Marine Division Headquarters.

The ride took about thirty minutes. I looked out the window as much as possible. That was kind of hard with the webbing in the way but I could see the South China Sea off to our right. It is actually part of the Pacific Ocean that ran from Singapore to the Strait of Taiwan. The

Vietnamese call it the Eastern Sea because the coast runs up the east side of the country.

The land stretched out green due to lush vegetation next to the ocean blue. Pockets of bomb craters were obvious and rice paddies with small villages dotted the landscape. Wherever the ground showed through, the earth was red due to all the clay. From above, Vietnam looked pretty peaceful with no active signs of war. But I knew it was dangerous on the ground.

As the KC-130 engines slowed, we knew we were landing. Now Phu Bai was a whole different story from Da Nang. It was originally set up as an Army communications installation and was more remote than Da Nang. It was a helicopter base and artillery base. Since it was so large, there was a huge enlisted men's club with a jukebox and a long bar.

I'd get to see all of that later. For now I checked out the runway, a grid of steel matting. Down either side of the runway, the matting had been built up into stalls to protect the aircraft from incoming mortar and rocket attacks. Different types of helicopters were parked inside these stalls, mostly CH-53 Sea Stallions and the CH-46 Sea Knights.

Both choppers were mainly used to transport troops and to re-supply units in the field. The CH-53 was larger and could transport approximately thirty-eight men; the CH-46 was long and slender and carried about seventeen Marines. The Huey UH-1Es were equipped with rocket pods on both sides. They also carried a pair of machine guns. The 2.75-inch rocket rounds could be real deadly, and the machine guns fired 7.62-mm rounds.

A few CH-53 Sea Stallions were parked on the runway, a couple with their rotors whirling. They were very loud and threw red dirt and dust everywhere. A couple of small, bubble-shaped helicopters were also there. One was just lifting off, taking a low altitude and skimming pretty fast over the runway.

Once I got out of the plane, I heard artillery fire, possibly from a fire mission. The number of outgoing rounds was a lot more intense than at Da Nang. On the ground, Vietnamese people were everywhere. They wore cone-shaped hats of tightly woven straw or bamboo to protect them from the sun and rain. Some of the younger ladies wore the Ao dai, a long dress that was Vietnam's national costume. They rode or pushed bicycles and walked to the base from every direction.

As a truck carried us toward the division headquarters, I wondered why so many Vietnamese people were on base. It turns out that most of them worked there, some at the PX or the mess hall, the men as barbers and the women at the laundry. The younger women worked at the exchange as clerks.

I hoped the base did a good job of screening people before they were allowed onto the base. The North Vietnamese Army (NVA) and VC ran a pretty intense propaganda campaign among the South Vietnamese people. A number of front groups operated throughout the area, and village leaders were often murdered and replaced with undercover NVA/VC operators. We constantly had to be alert to danger.

Our truck made a final turn and headed up the main street to division headquarters, slowing on the wet, dirt road. Old Glory flew high on a pole with the Vietnamese flag next to it. I was impressed by the headquarters area and looked forward to my tour of duty with the Third Division.

Chapter Five
Third Marine Division

The personnel office instructed me to report to the Headquarters Battalion transit area a few yards down on the other side of the street. A young sergeant there told me to pick up a poncho liner, cot, and items from supply then find a place to bed down for the night. After that, there wasn't much to do until chow time.

We shot the breeze, talked about all the Vietnamese walking around and what we thought of the country. Clouds gathered overhead and it seemed like it was going to rain. Since there was no formation for chow, we went to the mess hall to wait out front. As we stepped around puddles, we saw a long line of troops.

"What unit you guys with?" someone asked.

"We just arrived," I said. "We haven't been assigned yet."

"That means you're with Headquarters Company. The mess hall has certain times set aside for different companies to eat so they might not let you in now."

We stood around waiting until it was time for Headquarters Company to eat. You should have seen the stares we got. We were pretty clean compared to those Marines who'd just returned from the field. They wore jungle fatigues with camouflage boots and some carried their weapons; a few were wearing soft covers but some had helmets. A few of the helmets had all kinds of writing on them. And there we were with our semi-starched stateside green utilities and our spit-shined black leather boots.

One of the Marines said, "I smell a newbie." Everyone laughed.

After quite a bit of ribbing, we decided to head back to the transit area. It wasn't long before we returned to the mess hall to wait in line. Some of the same troops were still waiting but they didn't seem to care what unit we were with. They asked us a lot of question about the States.

"What songs are popular now?" one asked. "What kind of music is being played?"

Then somebody asked what the girls were wearing. "I heard miniskirts are all the rage," he grinned. "What do they look like?"

"That's nothing," we said. "The micro-mini was just starting to hit the streets when we left."

They all yelled when they heard about the micro-mini.

"Forty-five more days!" some shouted.

"Ninety days and I'll be home!" yelled others.

After the excitement died down, they gave us a rundown on how certain units operated in the field, explaining that some would see action while others wouldn't. The information would be pretty useful.

The mess hall was soon ready and we headed inside. They wished us luck as we worked down the chow line.

I guess the more experienced Marines wanted to haze us a little. We must have handled it well because they didn't give us any trouble the second time we showed up at the mess hall.

I tried to remember everything those guys said. It was like another kind of training. I learned plenty at boot camp, of course, and the day after graduation, some of my platoon continued on to MOS or Military Occupation School. Others, like me, were classified as Infantry (0311) so we headed to Camp Horno for specialized training.

The same thing had happened when my platoon graduated from boot camp. Suddenly the DIs treated us differently. When the DI told us to get our gear, he didn't yell at us. Since we had hung tough all through boot camp, we'd finally earned his respect.

We'd also earned the right to a few extra privileges. The DI said we could let our hair grow out a little so we wouldn't look like bald eagle chicks any more. Even the bus we rode up to Camp Horno was different. It had air conditioning and the seats were soft with high backs. Compared to the buses we'd been using, it felt like heaven.

Camp Horno was far past Edison Range and more inland. It sat down in a valley surrounded by huge hills or low mountains. After the bus made several turns, it stopped in front of a flat, single-story barrack. It looked like an open squad bay with plenty of windows and all of them were open. All the buildings were concrete with a gray finish, except a couple of metal warehouses.

Our training ran day and night. The majority were live fire exercises and familiarization with the crew serve weapons. Learning how to use the flame thrower was pretty neat. It was awesome to let loose with a squirt of the chemical gel while calling out, "Burn!" At night we trained on compass reading. Some teams got lost during those exercises and the instructor had to go find them.

The first day on the grenade range was a little strange. We had helmets and they gave us flak jackets but for some reason, I was still a little frightened.

"What if the grenade falls out of my hand?" I wondered.

"What if someone accidentally throws his grenade into my pit?" I had thoughts about weird things, things I shouldn't have been thinking.

But it turned out okay. I was actually amazed and shocked. I thought with all my experience in high school as a baseball pitcher, I'd be able to throw the grenade pretty far. I was wrong. The trick was in how the grenade was held. Although it is shaped like a baseball, it had to be held a certain way. Most importantly, it needed to land at least forty yards away. Otherwise the shrapnel might come back on friendly troops.

Despite all our training, in Phu Bai we stuck out like kids with shiny green clothes. The mess hall was packed and pretty loud...until we walked in. There was a pause as everyone looked at us. Although everyone went back to talking, we felt uneasy eating with the troops. We were different. Until we went out in the field, we just wouldn't fit in.

We wanted to finish our meals fast and get out of there. I can't even remember what I ate because I felt so out of place. The chow might have been our last decent meal for a long time. If we joined our unit the next day, we'd be eating C rations for a while.

I didn't relax until we carried our trays outside. Then it was just like in the States: scrape off the garbage here, dip the tray in a pot of hot water, and scrub it with a brush and then rinse. The only difference from the U.S. is that here the dishwashing pots were tended by the Vietnamese people.

Soon I'd get used to things. For now, though, everything was as new as the time I'd spent at boot camp. One day, when I would have my own field experiences, I would gain the respect of the other men who'd already been through their own combat experiences.

* * *

After breakfast the next day, we headed back to the transit area. We'd been assigned to a working party in Vietnam, of all places. Man, what a job. We picked up cigarette butts around the area. It only took us fifteen minutes so it wasn't too bad.

After that, we mustered in front of Headquarters Company office to receive our orders. I was assigned to the Second Battalion, Fourth Marines which has a long and illustrious history dating back to April 1914 during WWI when it was activated as one of the three battalions of the 4th Marine Regiment. In about an hour, a truck would take us to Camp Evans, up the road from Phu Bai. I'd heard about the Second Battalion, Fourth Marines and the operations they'd been involved in, including firefights in the Chu Lai area. I was already proud of that unit and I hadn't even joined them yet.

When the trucks arrived, they were already loaded with supplies. The driver said to climb on. I found a good spot toward the center of the truck just behind the cab. I settled down in a hole between the supplies where it gave me a little protection on all sides. We had no flak jackets, no helmets, and no weapons. I wondered, "What were we supposed to do if we got ambushed? Chuck C rations at them?"

As our convoy passed through the gate, I saw our protection. A helicopter gunship flew alongside us as our escort. The UH-E1 Huey's rocket pods were fully loaded. A couple of trucks mounted with .50 caliber machine guns on the cabs were also in the convoy; the convoy commander was leading the way up Highway 1 to Camp Evans.

We made several twists and turns through different villages. Most were surrounded by a bamboo fence. Inside the fence were thatched roof huts where people lived. Some had gardens and livestock like chickens, pigs, and ducks that wandered around. In some villages, people came out of their huts to watch us pass through. However, most of the time, they stayed inside because they were afraid.

A lot of peasants were walking or riding bikes on the roads. Women and men carried their goods over their shoulders or on their heads; some also had long poles with baskets of vegetables or water buckets at either end. Vendors had set up all along the road. Little children were everywhere with their tiny hands stuck out, begging. Our driver pitched some extra C ration candy to them and the kids scrambled for anything the Marines tossed down.

As we entered a large city, the driver yelled, "Hue City!"

Hue City's buildings were made of cement patterned like stucco and looked modern. Motorized vehicles and bicycles crowded the streets. The city was a beautiful sight. It felt like I was on a scenic tour. A huge citadel had a statue of either Jesus or the Virgin Mary; I don't remember which. It was pretty, though, and I wished I had a camera to take pictures so the family back home could see the beauty of Hue City.

Vendors again lined the streets and their shelves were stocked with Salem and Kool cigarettes. Hard liquor was everywhere, and some people were even selling C rations. I remember seeing a lot of very beautiful, young women, all dressed in those flowing gowns. Hue City would later be hit hard during the Tet Offensive in 1968. Tet is the Vietnamese New Year and while the South Vietnamese were out celebrating, the VC hit squads used that timeframe to launch a massive attack that would kill more than 2,800 unarmed government officials, school teachers, and intellectuals in that city alone.

Somehow, amid all the atrocities and bombs, life went on for the Vietnamese people. Out in the rice paddies, people stood knee-deep in water. The fields were plowed with water buffalo. I even saw a kid riding one. The buffalo had no problem pulling the plow, as a little old man would keep that huge animal moving with nothing more than a thin stick.

I'd only seen things like this in movies, yet there I was watching everything in person. I just could not believe I was in Vietnam, unarmed to boot.

* * *

After our sightseeing trip, we turned off Highway 1 and drove up a dirt road to Camp Evans. By then it was extremely hot, probably late morning. The trucks pulled up near some field tents strung with camouflage netting. While the clerks were getting things together inside, we sat around on sandbags outside introducing ourselves to each other.

Directly in front of the battalion headquarters some distance away loomed huge mountains. Since most of the good cropland was in the low-lying areas, not many people lived in the mountains. Instead the mountains were comprised of thick jungles filled with wild boars, monkeys, and snakes…lots of snakes.

A clerk came out and asked if anyone wanted to volunteer to be a tunnel rat. The VC had been ramping up for war for so long they'd created an extensive network of underground tunnels. They could hide men and supplies underground and even hole up for long periods until they got the chance to attack.

"What does a tunnel rat do?" one Marine asked.

"Underground search and destroy missions," said the clerk. "The tunnels are tight so you go in with only a .45 caliber pistol and a flashlight. Your duty will be to kill any enemy you encounter and plant explosives to destroy the tunnels."

The tunnels also had numerous booby traps. Deep bends might be flooded so that poisonous gas could be trapped on the other side. There were also snakes, spiders, and scorpions.

Both the Marine and I said, "No, way."

The clerk didn't seem surprised. He told me, "You're going to Golf Company, along with these others."

35

The seven of us grouped together. Another Marine with a rifle slung over his shoulder joined our group. He wore a flak jacket over a green T-shirt, and his trouser pockets were so stuffed with items that he bulged everywhere.

He took us to our company area just down the street, walking by rows of tents with the side flaps rolled up. Inside the tents were rows and rows of empty cots. The Marine pointed to one tent and told us to stage our gear there.

We checked in with the company office, got our 782 gear—a flak jacket, helmet, suspender straps, cartridge belts, two canteens, a cover with a canteen cup, a poncho, and liner. Then the armory gave us M-16s with bayonets and scabbards. The rifle was extremely light and actually looked like it was made of plastic. We also got four magazines, each of which held twenty 5.56-mm rounds.

We decided to stick close to each other and headed back to stage our 782 gear. Someone said to make sure we had the malaria and water purification tablets in our first aid kits. We'd also received lightweight jungle fatigue trousers with huge cargo pockets and matching jackets…but no jungle boots. The clerk said he'd issue the jungle boots only when our leather ones fell apart. That was pretty important because the canvas would dry out a lot faster than the leather in the jungle.

Even without them, though, we were beginning to look every bit like Marine warriors. We were instructed to wear our helmets and carry our weapons at all times, even when going to chow. We also picked up C rations for three days in case we needed to go into the field. We took the cans and food packets out of their boxes like little kids opening Christmas toys, stuffing everything into our field packs.

For some reason, the seven of us didn't want to stay in the company tents. We just didn't feel comfortable taking over someone else's area, especially since we were the new kids. Plus, we didn't want to be told to move if we accidentally took someone's spot. Besides, we were already comfortable sleeping on the ground.

We put our ponchos together and made a shelter to keep the hot April sun from beating down on us. Our shelter was large enough for all seven of us. We couldn't keep out the dust the helicopters kicked up but we made do. We even set up our own security watch to protect the equipment from vandals when we went to chow or were on work detail.

The seven of us got to know each other pretty quick. We learned where everyone came from, where we went to school, what level of education we had, what our parents did for a living, if we were married or had kids, and what we did before joining the Corps. After that initial introduction, we believed we could trust and rely on each other if anything happened.

During the night, the only requirement we were given was bunker watch on the battalion perimeter side of camp. The company had three bunker positions from which to stand watch but we manned only one. On my first watch, I looked out over a valley to the villages below. Even though the spot was surrounded by hedges, bamboo and other trees, the elevation gave me a perfect view.

I could hear children making playful noises. Smoke rose from the center of the villages and floated in the air. There was so much smoke, they must have been cooking dinner or burning trash. Late that evening I heard chanting, followed by a gong. Buddhism was the most popular religion and had come to Vietnam from India during the Chinese rule. They might have been having prayer service that night.

The gong seemed to go on until midnight. It might have ended sooner but it was easy to lose track of time out there. As I took it all in, I thought, "Welcome to Vietnam."

* * *

Later that same night, I saw a flash of lights several miles to the northeast. The flashes were from the B-52 aircraft based in Guam. They came all that way to drop 500- to 1,000-pound bombs in the DMZ.

The DMZ was the strip that partitioned North and South Vietnam. It separated the entire country into two military zones. Established by the Geneva Conference of 1954, the DMZ had initially been intended as a temporary demarcation. By the time I arrived in Vietnam, it might have been considered more permanent.

South Vietnam was thought of as the first domino in a series. If it fell to communism, the U.S. felt strongly that all of Southeast Asia would quickly follow. Hawaii and America's west coast wouldn't be far behind. Between that and the importance of the South China Sea as a shipping lane, Marines were fighting for America's freedom as much as for Vietnam's.

Arc lights skimmed through the darkness like fireworks on Independence Day. Further off in the distance, illumination flares lit the sky followed by tracer rounds from an AC-47 Dragon Ship, a propeller plane nicknamed Puff the Magic Dragon. Its three mini-guns fired 5,000 to 6,000 7.62-mm rounds per minute. Since every fifth round was a tracer, it looked like a dragon spitting fire. What a plane!

As I watched this night light show, I knew Puff was firing on the enemy. Every once in a while I heard outgoing artillery fire. Suddenly, someone yelled, "Fire the 106!"

The 106-mm recoilless rifle, or RCL, was extremely loud and put out a huge back blast. They were lightweight enough to be carried by a Marine yet fired a heavier projectile than could be handled with a recoiling weapon. They had been developed during WWII and were often used as anti-tank weapons.

Since the projectile could be seen traveling all the way down to its target, it was easy to watch it explode. I never understood how they could request a fire mission from the 106 since the projectile flew out flat. But when the call came, they had to do it. That night there was plenty of action to watch from my perch.

After the fire mission quieted down, everything went back to normal. The night was a sight to behold. The sky was clear and the stars were bright, shining, and twinkling above me. The gong had stopped and everyone bedded down for the night. Only a few dim lights could be seen here and there.

The remainder of the night was so peaceful one never would have known a war was going on. I still couldn't believe I was in Vietnam while history was being made. Just a week before, I'd been eating a cheeseburger in southern California. The entire experience seemed like a regular military training exercise even though I knew it wasn't.

When my shift ended, I told my relief to wake me early so I could see the sun rise over the rice paddies. As daylight approached, a rooster crowed in the distance. I couldn't tell if it came from the village or the mountain range. The sun peeked over the horizon, a beautiful yellow with a mixture of purple caused by the clouds.

When the rooster crowed again, it seemed to have moved location. The mountain tribes believed that everything—the forest, the clouds, the animals, and the rivers—had their own spirits, so maybe a ghost rooster was flying around the jungle. Soon the villagers started waking up and wisps of smoke rose from their thatched huts or hooches, as they were often called by the military.

Around 0600 hours I headed back to our man-made poncho shelter after being on watch. One of the guys talked with me about what had happened during my watch while we enjoyed the C ration coffee. Down in the villages, the Vietnamese were mixing pho, a noodle soup with beef broth, onions, and ginger for breakfast. Finally, I decided to get some shut-eye before the morning grew too hot.

Chapter Six
Golf Company

We stayed in the company area for eight days. Several attempts were made to fly us out on the CH-46 Sea Knight. The helicopter was narrow but long and could hit speeds up to 160 miles per hour. I really looked forward to the ride but each time our departure was cancelled due to lack of space or an inability to land in a certain landing zone (LZ).

Truthfully, it didn't bother us much. We were content to stay in the company area while we acclimated to the surroundings and Vietnam. The Vietnamese worked in the rice paddies each day. Watching entire families pitch in to plant and harvest rice, gather the tropical fruits, and work their gardens reminded me of my own life growing up in Oklahoma.

My family lived off the land as much as we could. We raised our own chickens and planted a garden every year. Mom grew a variety of vegetables and various types of beans. Mom always told Dad what she wanted long before spring arrived. Dad helped her plan the garden and later helped plant the seeds and onion bulbs. They were quite a team.

The first stage was tilling the field. Dad would solicit friends and neighbors for a team of plow horses or, if the garden was bigger, a tractor. Mom often planted row after row of sweet corn, green beans, okra, and various types of onions. Gardening provided great pleasure for Mom and provided food for the whole family.

In exchange for having the field plowed, she would give the driver fresh vegetables at harvest or a box of canned items from the year before. She was very good at preserving and canning vegetables, as well as making wild plum or blackberry jellies and jams. Every year she picked buckets of green beans, and red and green tomatoes.

She even made her own sauerkraut from the cabbage she grew but our favorite was her hot chow-chow. Chow-chow was a spicy relish made from tomatoes, hot peppers, onions, and spice. It made us feel warm inside, especially when eaten with a bowl of pinto beans, a plate of fried potatoes, and milk gravy.

I'm not sure how my mother made her gravy. Once in a while, though, she added a can of Pet Milk. Back then, that was a luxury. I believe she started out by melting bacon grease, then adding flour to form a paste, stirring all the time. Once she got a nice consistency, she added the milk and continued stirring. The amount of flour determined how thick or thin the gravy turned out.

Every harvest she slaved over the hot wood stove canning vegetables and other items all day for weeks so we'd have food for the winter. Since Dad couldn't work as much those months, we made do with what she had preserved. She also made soups and dumplings with the canned foods. Life back then consisted of two meals a day: a late breakfast and a late supper. Sometimes we had leftovers for supper, but sometimes we had pork chops with mashed potatoes and gravy.

Once, my sisters and I stopped on the way home from school at an empty house. The yard had two pear trees and the fruit was ready. I stuffed as many as I could in my shirt to take home but we ate a lot while we walked. My sisters ate so much they ended up with stomach aches that night. What fruit made it home was used to make cobbler for supper the next evening.

Sometimes we walked home using a trail through the pasture. We always stopped to pick any wild plums we found along the way. Sometimes we scouted around for blackberry patches. If we located one, Dad went the next day and picked a bucketful so Mom could bake blackberry cobbler. If a lot of berries were left over, she'd made jams or jellies.

Maybe that's why I'm pretty fond of blackberry cobbler today. Add a big scoop of vanilla ice cream and let it melt into the hot cobbler...now, that's good eating. My favorite, though, was Mom's hot buttermilk biscuits. I ate those with a pat of butter melted into the middle and topped with homemade jelly.

Two favorite staples among Native American Indians in the area where I grew up were wild grapes and wild onions. We probably could have survived solely on those two items since Mom knew what she was doing.

Wild grapes grew in the woods and alongside the roads. When they were ripe, we kids picked them and Mom cooked the grapes to extract the juice. She made grape dumplings from the juice she canned. The grape dumplings made your mouth and teeth purple but they were so good served hot, especially on cold days.

Once onions were gathered and cleaned, my mother quickly boiled them and popped them into a canning jar with some water. After sealing the lid, she boiled the whole jar. The jars were stored away under her bed and whenever we wanted onions we retrieved a jar from the cardboard box she used for storage.

For supper, we usually had wild onions cooked with eggs and served with red beans and rice, along with Mom's hot buttermilk biscuits. During the cold winter months we sat at the table with the wood stove blazing away behind us. Sometimes, she would make us fried potatoes and if we got tired of fried potatoes, Mom boiled the potatoes instead.

Another favorite dish of mine was her onion, tomato, and macaroni soup. For some reason that soup stands out in my mind; it had a lot of flavor. The soup was especially wonderful with day-old biscuits Mom deep-fried to a golden brown or toasted on top of the stove.

My family lived off the land as much as possible until Mom got to a point where she couldn't manage the garden anymore because of illness. She scaled back and made a smaller garden. She didn't can as much as she had. Mostly she made small items like her hot chow-chow and some jellies. She complained that her legs hurt a lot when she stood for long periods but promised that when she felt better, she'd do more canning. She was never able to, though.

I believe my mother was on the verge of her diabetes diagnosis then and we didn't realize it. She was tired a lot and just didn't feel like tending the garden. I think that was another reason why we moved to town, to ease her life as much as possible. As the result of her diabetes, she lost both legs later in life.

Halfway around the world watching the rice paddies being plowed and planted, I found that things were very different and also somehow familiar. All the new Marines were slowly getting a taste of Vietnam and there was still a thirteen month stretch ahead before we could go home.

* * *

The time for us to join our company finally arrived. The administration clerk told us to get more C rations and more ammunition if we

44

needed. We hadn't used the first issue so replenishing wasn't necessary. As we stocked up with new C rations, we all decided we liked the new packs, which were an upgrade from what we used in training. These were bigger, nylon packs that had more compartments so we could carry more items including up to five days of C rations and additional ammunition.

Still, we thought it best not to lug too much stuff into the field. We all decided to carry only extra socks and our ponchos. We also took plenty of heat tabs to make for hot chow and coffee. Then we cleaned our weapons so as not to make a bad impression on our first day in the field.

As we worked, one of the men suggested we make a vow to stay in touch with each other in case we were split apart into different platoons. We'd already grown so close that we agreed right away. We promised to stay in contact no matter what happened. We were forming our own Band of Brothers.

The next morning some men went to chow but others, including me, ate C rations and drank coffee. We knew it might be our last hot chow for a while but we didn't care; we were too anxious to get into the field. After tearing down our shelter, we waited in front of the company office. The clerk gave us several large yellow and orange nylon bags containing mail for the company. The troops would kill us if we lost those bags.

We headed to the helicopter pad. Several five-gallon water cans were stashed there, some plastic and others olive-drab gas cans with water printed on the side. C rations were stacked high on pallets. We loaded the supplies and boarded the CH-46 Sea Knight. It was extremely loud inside, and hand and arm signals were used by the crew chief manning an M-60 machine gun in the window.

We gave each other the thumbs-up to signal good luck. The pilot lifted off slowly and flew pretty low for a time. Then we picked up altitude and skimmed over a mountain range. Clouds or a lifting fog shrouded parts of the mountain and the jungle was a dark tangle underneath.

A few months before arriving in Vietnam, I had been promoted to lance corporal. I had been promoted while on active duty at the Marine Barracks in Bremerton, Washington. Now I had reached another milestone as a Marine. For the next thirteen months, Golf Company would be my home. I don't know if I qualified as real gung-ho but I was motivated to do my job the best I could. I would give it my all; it's what the Marine Corps calls Esprit de Corps.

The Sea Knight swept into a large circle around the LZ before it set down. We ran out the back end of the aircraft and sat in a defensive position, facing outward, until someone came for us. The gunnery sergeant led us to the command post (CP) where we again sat around while they figured out where each of us would go.

The seven of us were split up. We were scattered among the First, Second and Third Platoons. I was assigned to the First. "See you later," we said, "Keep in touch." Then we were off.

Someone from the First Platoon welcomed me to Golf Company. He gave me a quick rundown of what was happening that day and the night's activity. I met the platoon sergeant and the squad leaders, who were in for a briefing. "I'm supposed to get the next new man," one corporal said.

The platoon sergeant didn't argue. "He's all yours," he said.

When I reported to the squad, the men asked me a lot of questions about the States: what kind of music was popular, how certain baseball teams were doing, what was happening in other sports...all the same questions the troops at Phu Bai had asked.

Right off, I was made a fire team leader responsible for myself and three other people. The leader looked out for their welfare and passed information to them through the chain of command. Members of a fire team usually included the leader, an automatic rifleman, an assistant automatic rifleman, and a rifleman, but I was only assigned two other men.

The squad leader told me I might take over his position when he rotated out. He didn't have all that long left in Vietnam and was looking forward to going home to his wife. Unfortunately, I still had my leather boots while he was telling me this. They were clean and shiny, and he kept looking at them while he talked.

I don't know if he was just rubbing it in or if I lost track of what he was saying but suddenly I heard, "Saddle up!"

The company moved out. As we climbed the side of the mountain, I kept losing my footing. It had rained the night before and the ground was still soggy. My boots weren't the right kind and had no traction. I was slipping and sliding so much the other men had to assist me.

I was sure they thought I was a weakling. Actually, I was very fit. I had been stationed at Bremerton, Washington for nearly a year before shipping out to Vietnam. The mess cooks there were very good. To keep from packing on the pounds, I worked out during my days off and between duty hours. One of my regiments was lifting weights, which I enjoyed, and jogging around the shipyard.

When I'd first arrived at Bremerton, I'd asked the clerk where Marines went for a haircut. The barber shop was located right next door to the E-club. Only after my hair was trimmed did I feel ready for duty. A haircut might seem like a little thing but every aspect of a Marine's presentation played a role. In Washington, it was a haircut; in Vietnam, it was a pair of boots.

*   *   *

My primary duty at Bremerton had been as a security guard but I also performed other duties such as formal military burial details and community functions. For example, I pulled Ceremonial Honor Guard detail in the shipyard when they christened a ship. When the Battleship Missouri berthed in Bremerton, thousands of people came to visit. I had plenty of opportunity to tour the ship but I missed out.

I did see the surrounding country, though. A ferry went to Seattle and occasionally I'd hop on. The ferry was an old prototype with paddlewheels at the rear and steam bellowing out of the smokestack. It took an hour or so to cross the sound. Majestic Mount Rainer stood in the far distance covered with snow; at my feet spread the deep blue waters of Puget Sound.

The shoreline was dotted with beautiful log homes and white cottages surrounded by evergreens. I always thought, "How beautiful can America be?" Boats cruising across the waters made for a picturesque scene. During the Christmas holidays when all the lights were on and the landscape was covered with snow, the tall evergreens planted in neat rows along the sidewalks made for a picture-perfect view.

The downside was that during winter, the skies stayed cloudy and overcast for months. For me, that was not good. I loved sunshine. That entire winter, I believe the sun came out only two or three times. It was a lot different than the hot, dry Oklahoma country where I spent most of my life.

Vietnam combined the worst of both worlds: constant fog and humidity along with hours of burning sunshine. When I finally reached the top of that mountain, I turned to check out the view. It looked like I was standing in the clouds. In the valley below, grayish fog blanketed the treetops out to the horizon.

I don't remember how many mountains we climbed or how many rivers we crossed that day but it was one too many for me. My leather boots had no mercy. I slipped on muddy slopes, on rocks at the bottom of rivers, and I fell constantly. I even fell while coming out of the river. My boots were soaked through, making the bottom of my soles slick.

I sure was glad when we stopped for the night. It wasn't that I was tired physically; I was just tired of falling and miserable because of those leather boots. I told the squad leader what the clerk had said about waiting to replace them. He said he'd put in an order for size 10R regular jungle boots for me. I couldn't wait.

The platoon guide told everyone to dig in; that meant make a fighting hole. A fighting hole had to be dug deep enough to shield at least one man and sometimes two. It was usually three to four feet deep depending on the terrain. We routinely dug single holes. Word was passed that a water run would take place soon and if anyone wanted a bath that would be our chance. A patrol was sent out to set up security around a nearby stream. We'd could refill our canteens and be able to wash knowing we wouldn't be ambushed by any VC.

It was good to clean up. It was also a mistake on my part because I had to take off my clothes. I had the whitest legs of all the men and was the only one still wearing the standard issue white boxers. Everyone got a good laugh at me.

Out in the field, underwear was a hindrance. It constrained whenever we climbed a hill, and when we lie on the ground to wait or sleep, it bound up in the most uncomfortable places. The corporal said not to worry about the hazing, as every man had gone through the same routine when first arriving in country. The experience helped build morale and camaraderie.

I did throw away those white skivvies, though. I ripped those drawers up pretty good and hid them under some big rocks by the stream. If a VC found them, he would probably put them to good use as a bandage. For my part, that was the last time I wore underwear the entire tour.

When I received two canteens full of water, I noticed right away that they weren't my canteens. Unless they were marked, chances were I wouldn't get the same ones back whenever we re-supplied our water. It didn't really matter so long as I had some water.

I dug into my first aid kit and dropped a water purification tablet into each canteen. The training at Camp Pendleton taught me how to judge the safety of the water sources we'd find. The stream was running pretty fast and the water was clear, so one tablet was probably enough.

Chapter Seven
Fire Team

With our constant movements through the jungle and across rivers and streams, it took less than a week for my leather boots to split and the soles to wear. If we didn't get re-supplied soon I'd be barefoot. I guess someone must have heard me because a CH-46 helicopter came in at an LZ we prepared.

Out came the orange and yellow mailbags followed by large boxes. Minutes after the CH-46s took off, mail was handed out. Some of the men received small packages. The platoon also got a box called the special package or SP, which was full of every brand of cigarettes, cigars, and chewing tobacco we could want.

I thought that if some of the guys didn't want their share, I could send a little home to my Dad. He'd taken such good care of my whole family all his life. When I grew up and started working myself, I took every opportunity to give a little back to my parents.

Although my family was large, all my siblings never lived at home at the same time. My oldest sister, Hattie, got married early and moved into town. My two older brothers, Jackson and Lewis, went to a boarding school, as did an older sister, Ramona. This left me and two younger sisters, Annie and Bessie, at home during most of my childhood.

Both my sisters were cute with light skin tones. Annie had long hair and was quiet and shy. Bessie had short hair and was outgoing with a good sense of humor. After school, we walked home together along a gravel road. No matter what the weather, we walked to and from school.

Sometimes, when we had a car that worked, Dad drove us but that was a rare treat. We entertained ourselves by throwing rocks at cans or glass bottles we lined up on fence posts. The first to knock them off or break a bottle won bragging rights at the dinner table that night.

Around the time I was in the third grade, my younger sisters and I were sent to boarding school. Although my older siblings had gone to Sequoyah in northeast Oklahoma, we went to Jones Academy. Located about a hundred miles from home, the academy was near the Sans Bois Mountains and Robber's Cave in eastern Oklahoma. The entire area was beautiful that fall.

The buildings, dormitories, and dining hall were nestled among tall oaks that bustled with gray squirrels. The boys' dormitory was the biggest building on campus. Steps led up both sides at the front of the white building and a long concrete balcony spanned the entire length. The older boys stayed on the third floor.

Buses from the Hartshorne Independent School District transported us five miles from Jones Academy to Hartshorne so we could attend school. The campus was huge and had two first-, second-, third-, and fourth-grade sessions running at the same time. When school let out at 3 each afternoon, we'd board the buses and head back to Jones Academy.

On Saturdays, I relaxed, played, and studied. On Sundays, everyone attended a church service in Hartshorne. Despite the impressive campus and weekends off, boarding schools weren't for everyone. Boys and girls were always running away. Why they ran away wasn't clear to me. The school gave us a nice place to stay and three hot meals a day.

I was only there for the first half of the academic year, though. Mom became ill. Since Dad was away working a lot, she needed someone to help around the house. I felt bad that my younger sisters had to stay at the academy while I headed home. Mom taught me how to cook and bake then, and I've always remembered how happy and proud she was that I could take care of her.

Later I had an opportunity to help my parents in a very different way. After high school, I moved to Oklahoma City to be near my brother and to find work. The city was the place to be for good jobs.

The area was busy and was experiencing a lot of new growth when I arrived. The government was tearing down skid row and renovating the downtown section. I liked the summer nights, primarily because of the softball games held in the park. There were games every night and anyone could participate. Playing softball to me was better than going to the rows of downtown bars where some Native Americans I knew would gather and drink.

Life wasn't easy; starting wages were low at $1.25 an hour. I worked at a company making aluminum screen doors and windows. Every pay period, I bought groceries for my parents. I didn't have to but I wanted to. My brother drove me to the supermarket and then home to Konawa.

With the groceries loaded in the trunk and his family loaded into the car, we all headed to Mom's house. About ten miles from home, my brother would pull over at a convenience store to pick up a couple six packs of cold beer. We knew Dad might want one because he always liked to cool off in the summer with a cold beer but he could never afford it. He always said, "Cold beer, cold beer, more beer," then laughed.

By that time, my parents had moved out of the little two-room house into this place we called the Big House. It had six huge rooms with three bedrooms located on the left. The massive front porch was tangled with morning glories climbing up both sides. There was also a big front room, a dining room, and a medium-size kitchen with a large wood-burning stove. Although the house had wooden shingles, the roof still leaked when it rained.

There was a chicken coop in the back of the house. My mother's chickens were mainly red. At one time, she purchased white pullets, barnyard chickens, for eggs for us to eat. And the bathroom was still out back. There had been a well in the yard but that eventually went dry. An old smokehouse and a huge wooden barn with a small corral sat nearby until a tornado hit.

Konawa is noted for having more tornadoes than anywhere else in Oklahoma. In fact, it has nearly three hundred percent more tornadoes than anywhere else in the U.S. We were lucky we hadn't been home at the time. Our lives were spared, but financial hardship kept us from rebuilding the barn or replacing everything.

When my brother turned onto the long driveway during our weekend visits, we could see our parents sitting on the front steps. My brother always got out first and offered Dad a can of cold beer. In our native language Dad would say, "Hmmm! You know, I was just thinking about a cold beer and wished I had one on a day like today."

As I unloaded the groceries, Mom was always very excited to see what I bought. She'd sign, "Thank you." They were always running low on just about everything so it was a priority of mine to bring them food. Mom would give me a big kiss as we started into the house. Once inside, she drew the number 100 on the wall with her finger to show that I'd passed.

Later, Mom fixed a nice meal, always making hot biscuits and gravy. I don't think Dad could have survived without those at every meal. He always told my brother and me to eat but we always ate before arriving home. Dad would laugh and say in our native language, "Ho hum, didn't save me any."

After he ate, we sat around and talked about what was going on in the community while he enjoyed his cold beer. I also made it a habit to get Dad his tobacco; his favorite was Day's Work. Sometimes I'd get him a couple of packs of Beech Nut chewing tobacco; he seldom smoked cigarettes.

They were good parents and I tried to help them as much as possible. They gave me life and hope, so that was my way of honoring them. During these trips, my brother and I always went fishing the next day. Dad would tell us where to go, sometimes to spots we weren't familiar with.

The following morning, Dad would be up early digging night crawlers with us to use for bait. After almost filling a coffee can with bait, we'd go back inside and wash up to eat breakfast. Dad always went along with us. He didn't fish but he liked to watch and keep us company. We'd catch catfish, perch and bluegill. Sometimes we'd go hunting for rabbit or squirrel.

After a short weekend, we'd head back to the city late Sunday afternoon. That had been my routine just about every other weekend. Even with the love I felt for my family, I couldn't live like that anymore. I was twenty years old. I needed to find a trade or attend a technical school to get one. I wanted to better myself so I could earn a decent wage.

Even in Vietnam, with a job that made my whole family proud and the beginnings of a career in the military, I was still thinking of little things I could do to help my parents. I kept a pack of cigars from the SP package to smoke later. Plus, I still had tobacco I brought from home. I only smoked every now and then, so it lasted quite a while.

Then I was handed a package. My first pair of jungle boots had come just in time. I felt like a kid opening up a Christmas gift. They were a good fit, and I also got new socks. Now I looked like a real Marine warrior from top to bottom...and underneath, without the skivvies!

We dug in for the night. While we settled in, I heard that same ghost rooster crowing. Word came down that we could light up, which meant we could use our heating tablets to warm up our C rations. A heat tab is blue, about the size of a silver dollar, and a quarter to a half inch thick, wrapped in foil. After opening the heat tab, it was set in a portable stove and lit. The flame usually lasted just a few minutes so you had to move fast if you wanted hot food.

As long as we were firing up the heat tabs, we could also smoke. At these times I used the tobacco package given to me by a medicine man before I left home. During my thirty-day leave in Oklahoma City before shipping out, I ran into an older cousin.

"Have you seen a medicine man yet?" she asked. "You need protection, especially if you're going into combat. The medicine will keep you safe."

She arranged for me to see one before I shipped out. If the medicine man couldn't meet with me, she said she'd get something for me to take along.

I hadn't thought about getting medicine because I really wasn't expecting to go to Vietnam. I didn't know very much about the conflict and didn't understand how fast things were moving. But things always have a way of working out.

Less than a week after our conversation, my cousin came over to my brother's house and gave me a small package. The medicine man had made up a tobacco mixture, and my Dad gave me a pipe. I kept the container in my backpack inside a plastic bag to keep it dry. I used the mixture whenever we were allowed to smoke.

The medicine man had said to believe in it, to safeguard it, and to use it according to his specific instructions. That meant keeping away from other Marines whenever I smoked. I also had to fan the smoke over me with my free hand. I didn't smoke the tobacco mixture every time an opportunity to light up was offered but if I wanted to, I did.

It was a nice evening sitting on that mountain, cloudy but nice. Since we'd made great time on our patrol, we were able to sit around and talk while we fixed our meals and ate. It actually felt like camping out with all the stories being told.

* * *

One summer, my cousin and I slept out under the stars. Oklahoma summers were pretty hot, especially in July and August, and the house didn't ever seem to cool off inside. We often slept outside since it was so much cooler. During one of my sleepovers, we lay out on an old truck bed my uncle had converted into a sleeping platform. It was under a tree and had a thick mattress.

We counted as many shooting stars as we could before we fell asleep. It must have been in the early '60s because the Russians had just put Sputnik into space. We lay there trying to track its path. It was always amazing what else crossed the skies at night. We wondered what it would be like to travel in space or just to be able to fly a jet. We always said that if we joined the Air Force, we'd be pilots.

We talked a lot about what we wanted in life and how we wanted to live. The first thing we both always said was that we wanted to help our parents. I told my cousin I wanted a large ranch with cattle and horses like our grandfather had in the old days. I'd turn it over to my

Dad to do the hiring and he could supervise the work hands. I would get him a nice hay-hauling truck like he'd always wanted and a nice car.

The vehicle of choice back then was either a Cadillac or Lincoln Continental. I dreamed of pulling up to a gas station, saying, "Fill it up." No more buying fifty cents or a dollar's worth of gas at a time. My cousin and I wanted the same good life for both our parents; they were our priorities.

It's a good thing I was able to enjoy those little moments back home while I was in Vietnam. I had another year of duty ahead of me.

* * *

After a week, it was my turn to take my fire team out. The men assigned to me were both Caucasian with blond and sandy hair. They were about average height and weight, and both as young as I. The average age of American Marines in Vietnam was nineteen but we all had that Marine training under our belts. We were ready to serve.

Our task was to set up a listening post (LP) several yards outside the company perimeter. We were still in the mountain so they gave us a radio, the PRC25. While we waited for the night to get dark enough, we double-checked the frequency, call signs, and squelch mode so the radio wouldn't make much noise. Then we had chow and packed just enough equipment to sustain us for the night.

Finally it was time to move out. I got the team together, checked the radio once more, and headed to our position. The company radio operator would call for a situation report (sit-rep) every hour. To help us maintain cover, we couldn't respond by talking. Instead we'd key our handset twice to indicate that everything was okay.

We settled into a dry streambed with plenty of cover. From that position, we could listen for VC activity without being seen. Our watch ran from 2200 to 0500 hours. Each of my men was assigned a two-hour watch and I took the final watch of three hours. The task to secure the LP watch was simple but being separated from the camp made it dangerous.

We were all dog-tired and could be asleep in seconds. It seemed like I'd just put my head down for some shut-eye when the second watch woke me. I grabbed the radio receiver and sat listening to the chatter. I thought my turn had come up awfully quick. I suspected the men had moved the time up because it was still dark at 0600 hours. Normally, sunrise would occur around 0600 hours.

After securing our LP watch, we headed back inside the perimeter. "Did either of you guys change the watch?" I asked.

I knew they would say no but I asked anyway. They both denied tampering with the watch. Unfortunately, I didn't have a watch myself but when I asked the squad leader the time, I wasn't surprised that we were off by an hour. The pair had changed the watch and cut my sleep short.

What a group. And I was stuck with them until a rotation came along.

The good thing was that it never happened again. Maybe since I'd said something, they figured they couldn't get away with it again. Maybe they realized that we were in this together and we had to pull equal weight no matter how tired we were. Besides, even with this little trick, I knew they were good men. I just went with the flow and tried not to let the small things bother me.

* * *

The days and weeks went by pretty fast. I walked point once during a day patrol. I remember it was very hot. The thing I remember most, though, was that I was fortunate because nothing happened. The point man always had to be extremely cautious. I tried not to walk so fast I got separated from the main group and not so slow that we'd be ambushed.

There was also the constant threat of booby traps. Trip wires that set off grenades or other explosives might be strung along the trail and land mines were always being buried during the night. One anti-personnel mine was called the Bouncing Betty. When stepped on, the pressure released a mechanism that made the mine bounce up. The explosion then had a wider range and could blow off legs or mangle torsos.

The VC would set anything to harm our troops. They often made booby traps from materials they found. Foot traps were loaded with sharpened bamboo stakes and could inflict serious injuries to a foot and leg if stepped on. Even empty C-ration cans were turned into makeshift grenades by loading them with explosives.

The trees themselves could become weapons. A spiked mud ball could be loaded onto a sapling that could be released with a trip wire. The weight of the mud and the force of the tree springing back could impale a Marine. The traps and mines were so numerous they slowed the pace of American troops and caused a lot of terror for the local Vietnamese.

My biggest concern was punji stakes. They stuck up out of holes and could inflict a lot of damage. Most were laced with urine or human waste. Even if the puncture didn't seem bad, the bacteria could cause infection and lead to gangrene. In the time spent waiting for a medical evacuation helicopter, Marines could lose a foot or leg. Calling in a medevac right away would have slowed the mission so we kept a sharp eye out for the punjis.

To detect land mines, specialty Marines swept the rural roads with miniature metal detectors. Out in the jungle, though, the point man had to watch for land mines. He looked for piles of leaves or grass or dirt that had a different color, which meant it might have been recently disturbed. He also had to keep an eye on the surrounding bush in case of an ambush.

After my turn walking point, I saw my first casualty in the company. We were still in the mountains and had strung out as we moved through the area. Third Platoon was providing point that day. The company wound around the bend of the stream when a shot rang out. It was an AK-47, the standard VC/NVA infantry weapon.

The AK-47 has a certain sound that was nothing like our M-16 rifles so I knew it was the enemy. The shot was far ahead, and was the only rifle fire I heard. The point man had been climbing the embankment when he'd been hit in the chest. The point element immediately advanced to take a shot at Victor Charlie but he was gone. We referred to the VC as Victor Charlie.

The corpsman did everything in his power to save the young Marine but the battle ended badly. It was a tragic loss. The entire company felt the death of this one man. We were all pretty low, and asked each other about the Marine and wondered who was next.

A chopper was called to evacuate the body. The company set up security around the stream bed for the LZ. It took almost an hour for the CH-46 to arrive with its escorts. As the Huey gunship circled above, yellow smoke was thrown out to mark the LZ. It didn't take long for the chopper to pick up the Marine and leave.

We lost a couple hours of daylight taking care of our fallen brother but it was worth it. As soon as the chopper left, I heard, "Saddle up."

We adjusted our packs and continued our patrol. Extreme caution was on all of our minds because we knew Victor Charlie was out there somewhere. No one wanted to give him the luxury of harming us again.

Chapter Eight
Corporal

Sometime after that incident, one of our point men from Second Platoon surprised an NVA officer. He happened to be coming down the same mountain trail the company was heading up. When our point man rounded a bend, the two came face to face. Luckily, our guy was quicker on the draw.

"You should have seen the NVA soldier," the Marine said later. "He had this surprised look on his face and it seemed like his whole body froze."

That was all our guy needed to shoot first. After the platoon commanders examined the NVA, they determined he was a payroll officer. He was carrying a lot of cash and wore a star on his brown cap. He also carried a pistol. Someone took the cap but the pistol was retrieved by the commanding officer's (CO) staff for intelligence in our battalion area.

Knowing what the enemy forces had was important. The AK-47s and Soviet SKS carbines they used were a more than equal match to what the American troops were using. Unfortunately, their rifles were also more reliable and easier to maintain than the early version of the M-16. I would find that out firsthand during an upcoming firefight in September.

And just as the VC/NVA could rig very dangerous booby traps with what they found around them, they also had small workshops hidden in the jungle where they reloaded rifle cartridges and grenades. Their use of land mines was so extensive it was an effective replacement for their weaker artillery. So one officer less meant not only a reduction in their manpower but more intel for our side.

Still, it had been a close call. As we continued up the trail, each of us had to step over the dead NVA officer. Two incidents involving our point men reinforced the idea that I had to count my blessings each day.

* * *

A couple of days later we secured an LZ while another group of Marines trampled down the tall elephant grass. No one wanted to start a fire when the yellow smoke flare was thrown out. The area was deep in a valley with mountains on every side. The CH-53s were going to pick up the platoon and return us to Camp Evans.

Those troop carriers could be heard coming from a distance; they put off a very loud hum, not like the CH-46's clopping. Each helicopter came in with its tail slightly down. A platoon ran out and boarded; then another CH-53 landed behind the first and another platoon boarded. As soon as the first two lifted off, in came another two.

While the helicopters landed and lifted off, Huey gunships circled to provide protection. Once the troops were on board, the choppers always paused for a moment before lifting off. I always hated that pause. Every Marine had heard stories of choppers getting shot down at the LZs or being mortared while preparing to lift off. We were okay on this flight. It didn't take long before we descended inside the Camp Evans perimeter.

It was great being back. Some weeks had passed since I'd first left Camp Evans. I'd survived my first big patrol. I was looking forward to any mail and some hot chow but Marine Corps chores came first. We had to clean our weapons and wipe down our 782 gear. With all Vietnam's humidity and the frequent rain in the mountains, our rifles had to be cleaned more often.

Overall, it was nice to be sitting on my soft cot cleaning my rifle. I felt forty pounds lighter when I took off the field pack and flak jacket. I enjoyed listening to the old salts, the Marines with more time in country. Everyone laughed when they told jokes or told stories on each other about different field incidents. The chatter gave us a chance to regroup and think about things so we could avoid making potentially fatal mistakes in the future.

It was just like when I was younger, learning by listening to my folks talk. During meals, we sat around the table visiting and telling jokes. After my family's late suppers, my parents would talk about the good old days. We always moved out to the front porch and settled in. Once everyone was comfortable, out came the can of Prince Albert tobacco. My uncle rolled his own cigarettes while my Dad put tobacco in his pipe.

My parents usually started out with weather expected for the next day, followed by how it was causing them more aches and pains. Then they would move on to the home grown remedies, the "medicine" they used. My uncle would comment that he hadn't seen a certain plant in a long time. My Dad would say he'd found something else that worked just as well.

Then the fun began. Talking in our native language, each tried to out-do the other with their stories. I laughed at the things they talked about, and often wondered if what they said really happened the way they told it. I guess it didn't matter because I learned about how the family came to Oklahoma. Then they would get on a roll talking about myths and other things. I took everything in so I could pass the stories on to the next generation.

They talked a lot. If only they would have slowed down! Once they started a conversation, the adults talked a hundred miles an hour. My cousin and I just sat there, asking questions—if we could—between all their talking. When we did manage to ask something, they'd go at it again with different stories and different jokes.

During the winter we sat around the pot-bellied wood stove to talk while someone passed around a pack of cigarettes. We watched the flames through the openings on the top and front, laughing and shooting the breeze. The room was usually pretty dim. The kerosene lamps didn't put out much light, especially in a large room. We had only three lamps for the whole house; one was in the kitchen so Mom could see what see was cooking, one was in the dining area, and one was in the bedroom.

It felt like heaven.

* * *

When the company had a formation, a briefing was usually given on what we did, where our next mission would be, when we'd leave, and how we would get there.

The CO didn't give us much information, though. He just said we'd done a good job and to keep up the good work. We'd get word when our next assignment came down but for now we should rest.

I started writing letters home. Some Marines kicked back but all of us tried to stay out of the sun. We rolled up the sides of the tents so the breeze could come through. Not only did we get a little breeze, we also got a lot of dust from the choppers on the helipad. That didn't bother me. It felt good to snooze with that breeze on my face.

Evenings were a little different. Chow was at 1630 with a briefing by the platoon sergeant and squad leader a few hours later. We'd also have a quick class on maps and compass readings. After that, we stood in line for beer and sodas. Both were stashed in a small trailer covered with canvas. On those hot evenings, it was nice to have a cold drink of anything. I always thought of my Dad when he would say, "Cold beer."

I also remembered how my Mom always mimicked drunken people and told us kids not to make fools of ourselves. Mom was always very sentimental, especially when things didn't go right, but she had a great sense of humor and was always full of laughs. She continuously teased and joked with her kids and grandchildren. If we looked sad, she cheered us up by making us laugh.

Her humor didn't stop at teasing. She was also good at imitating people. As a game, she'd try to describe a person she just met. Her body language and facial expressions would mimic the person. Then she'd ask if we knew who she meant. If we didn't, she'd go into a longer routine, imitating their walk and dancing around. Plenty of times we said we didn't know who she was talking about just to see what she would do next.

She was very good at imitating intoxicated people. These charades made us laugh the most. Normally her antics kicked up after someone came to the house to see my Dad, often to borrow money. At times they reeked of alcohol, stumbled around, and drooled and slobbered when they talked. It actually made my mother sick.

The next day we'd ask who came to the house. Then she started acting like that person, making ugly faces by squeezing her lips and eyes and doing anything she could to get her point across.

Not only did she amuse us, we also got the message. If we drank, we were to be careful not to overindulge or else we'd look stupid, just like the people she imitated. Then she would pat us on the head and give us blessings.

In case I forgot this wisdom, the same message was sent during Stomp Dances, big social occasions put on by the Seminole every year. Just before dawn they'd have the last dance, the Drunk Dance. The first time I saw it, I thought it was a comic show. A couple of men dressed up in women's clothes then paraded around the arena. They looked for their mates, guys dressed up in raggedy clothes pretending to be drunk. They stumbled around the arena trying to hide from their beloved "wives."

I certainly didn't want to make a bad impression on my first trip back to Camp Evans so I always drank soda. I'd either give my beer to someone else or exchange it for another soda. There would be plenty of time to drink beer later. Often I gave my beer to one of the old salts. They had been in Vietnam longer and I thought they deserved it more than anyone else.

Beers I hadn't seen in ages got passed around. Pabst Blue Ribbon, Schlitz, and Carlin Black Label all made the circuit, and I bet they really had a kick. I saw a lot of two-beer Charlies, men who talked trash or went crazy after only a couple cans. Some of us laughed but we always took care of them. We put them to bed if they got too rough.

In a way, I was acting like a big brother to these guys. My own brothers had taken care of me the same way, even when I'd misbehaved. My two older brothers and one older sister attended an Indian boarding school at Sequoyah, Oklahoma, while I was still very young. I loved them dearly and didn't want to be left behind. I cried so much my parents lied to the officials about my age. I was only five years old but I felt like such a big kid because I got to go to school.

That was around 1949 or 1950. My oldest brother, Jackson, was fifteen and Lewis was a couple of years younger. Both my brothers had typical Indian features with dark hair and dark eyes. They were also good looking and always wore Levi trousers rolled up at the bottom. Jackson was quiet and shy while Lewis was more outgoing.

Ramona was around ten when she went to boarding school. She was short and had short hair. She was only at Sequoyah for a limited time. She contracted tuberculosis and was moved to a hospital in another town. While she was there, though, she always checked on me whenever we ran into each other at the cafeteria or social gatherings.

Sequoyah was nicely landscaped with winding roads. Near the entrance to the property was the football field and a red brick building for the faculty. There was also a brick four-story dormitory for girls age six to twelve and a two-story dorm for girls thirteen and up. Boys thirteen and up were housed in three tan buildings that looked like duplexes. The younger boys were housed in a white wooden building with three stories.

The campus also had a shop building, art building, cafeteria, and of course, classrooms. Children from all tribes attended the school, and they came from Oklahoma and other states. Students got breaks just like in normal schools and could go home if they had transportation. I only went home during the summer break.

Of course, I was the youngest and smallest kid on campus. That didn't bother me but my brothers had to look after me every now and then. I got pretty darn lonesome at that school so they'd come babysit me. Several times they smuggled me back to their rooms. They would give me candy and talk to me in our native language. Next thing I knew, they would threaten to send me home if I didn't straighten up.

After that, they didn't come to my dormitory during the night except when the house matron called them because I was crying. They sat by my bed and talked to me in our native language until I fell asleep. My brothers argued with each other about who was going to watch Sonny that night. When morning came I was always fine, just as if nothing had happened.

During the days I had it made. Since I was the smallest kid there, I got to march ahead of everyone else, especially when we went to the dining hall. The young ladies carried my tray and filled it with a little of everything. When I was done eating, I'd raise my hand and they would carry my tray back to the dishwashing station.

In the classroom, the teacher let me wander around the room. I'd usually end up sitting in the corner playing by myself. When recess came, I played with everyone else. The other students called me Governor because I had privileges they could never hope to have. I attended Sequoyah intermittently for about three years.

In Vietnam I was forming bonds with the men around me. They were becoming my brothers.

My day for trash-talking would come soon enough. I had lots of time to gain new experiences in the field. Right then, I enjoyed what I had — a little peace of mind and my newly found Band of Brothers.

* * *

The next morning I heard that ghost rooster again. As I went to the head — the bathroom — I saw a lot of the men still sleeping in the tents with the sides rolled up. Some guys were sprawled on the ground propped against their field packs. Some lie awake on their cots. They looked peaceful, just daydreaming and minding their own business. Needless to say, the men who'd partied the night before didn't feel like going to morning chow.

This was very different than my first morning at boot camp had been. At boot camp, you were required to go to morning chow. You didn't have a choice.

I remember flying to California for boot camp in the afternoon and marching late into the evening and until early the next morning. It seemed like I'd just put my head down on my pillow when the bugler sounded reveille. Since I was a light sleeper, I got up and made my bunk in the dark.

Some of the recruits, including me, were already dressed when a loud banging noise sounded on the door. The DI busted in and turned on the lights screaming, "Get out of the racks! Get out of the racks, you turds!"

One of the recruits was still lying in his rack. When the DI told him to get up, it was almost comical...almost.

"I don't eat breakfast," the recruit said. "Come back and get me when everyone's finished eating."

You could have heard a pin drop. The DI's face turned beet red and I thought, "Oh, no."

From that point, it almost seemed like things happened in slow motion. The DI grabbed the recruit's mattress and yanked. The private flew out of bed and rolled onto the concrete floor like an earthquake had hit.

"What's your name?" the DI demanded.

"Jones," the guy stammered.

The DI yelled at him for a long time using the recruit's name over and over. He finally called him a clown. "The rest of you!" he yelled. "Be dressed and on the street in fifteen minutes!"

He walked out and soon we heard the DI yelling inside the next hut.

"Lord have mercy," I mumbled.

We were all in shock. We dared not even look at the private still sprawled on the ground in his mess. We stepped over him, his mattress

71

and his linens to get to the head. Needless to say, Jones got dressed in a hurry and joined the rest of us.

"Jones," one of the other privates said. "What made you say you don't eat breakfast? You could have been killed!"

Then he started joking to break the ice. No one else was talking; we were all scared. When we finished, we ran through the hatch back to our Quonset hut and finished getting dressed. Jones made up his bunk and joined us for breakfast after all.

* * *

It was May 1967, and I'd been in country almost a month. One of the administration clerks said, "They're going to promote you along with some other Marines. You got the cutting score for corporal."

During my duty at Bremerton, Washington, I completed some Military Correspondence Institute (MCI) courses and I guess that was paying off.

The squad leader found me a little later and told me the good news. He didn't realize I already knew and I didn't let on that I knew. He told me to shave what whiskers I had and gave me some corporal chevrons. I brushed the dirt off my fatigues and polished my jungle boots.

At 1300 hours, the company marched out and centered themselves with the commander. The warrant for each promotion was read.

The ritual came afterward to pin the chevron to my shoulder. As was tradition, guys in my company would come by and punch me on the shoulder. I was black and blue for a couple of days from being punched there by so many of the guys but it was worth it.

Being promoted in South Vietnam was one of the happiest days of my life.

Chapter Nine
Spearheading the Battalion

My fire team and I made an odd bunch. One Marine had very bad eyesight. Every time he looked at something he had to squint. When I asked him if he had glasses, he said, "Yeah but they're back in the rear." That wasn't doing him or us much good.

The other Marine was hard of hearing. He said it was caused by being inside the helicopters. He heard whistling sounds all the time and had ringing in his ears. And there I was, a Native American Indian from a small town in Oklahoma, in charge of these two. We made quite the combination!

Once when the battalion was on an operation in the mountains, we'd worked our way down to the lowlands after being re-supplied. Golf Company took the lead with First Platoon walking point. My team was assigned to walk point for the night movement.

My instructions were to move several meters out in front of the battalion. The trail we traveled included an old railroad crossing over a deep ravine. There were no handrails and the ties were far enough apart to trip a misplaced foot. My mission was to set up a rope bridge so the battalion could cross safely in the dark.

They handed me some rope and I went back to brief my team. I think I scared them when I said we would be far ahead of the battalion in this march to no-man's land. Nightfall came pretty quick. We had on our war paint, our camouflage face paint, and we were loaded down with extra gear.

I had the rope, an extra can of 7.62-mm ammo for the machine-gun team, and my own M-16 with extra rounds. The Marine with poor eyesight was carrying a can of 7.62-mm machine-gun rounds in each hand and had slung his own weapon over his shoulder. The guy who had trouble hearing carried three light antitank weapons, or LAWs, a single-shot launcher which fires a 66-mm rocket. He also had an M-79 grenade launcher and extra 40-mm rounds for himself.

Even though we were careful to tie everything down, we all rattled so much. I wasn't sure who was going to walk point; it seemed like everything we learned in infantry training went out the door. We had a twenty-minute head start so off we went into the darkness on a trail leading to somewhere in South Vietnam. We were to have no radio contact with the battalion much less with the company. If we ran into the enemy, we were on our own.

The only safe thing about our mission was that to our right, illumination flares were going off in the distance near the coast. With that little bit of light, we could see silhouettes and objects ahead of us. The mountains to our left were pretty dark. As we continued, the wind picked up, blowing through the trees, brush and tall grass, rustling and whispering.

We stopped every now and then to listen but the only thing I heard was the rattle of our equipment. We tried to minimize the noise by not walking too fast. We moved out again, stopping and squatting periodically to see if anything was ahead. We couldn't stop too often as the battalion was only twenty minutes behind us. They expected us to have the rope bridge set up before they arrived.

We finally reached our destination. The team crossed to check both sides of the ravine for danger. Once the area had been secured, we strung a couple of ropes across the railroad trestle and sat out of view in case Victor Charlie strolled by.

As we waited for the battalion, my mind played tricks. "What will I do if a VC approaches?" I wondered. "It would come down to him or me."

Then I thought, "What if they kill me? How will my parents take it?"

The other Marines were across the ravine. They wouldn't be able to help me if something happened. Worse yet, what if those two were killed or even captured in a firefight on their side?

"What would I do, what was my chance of survival, how would I explain something like that to the platoon?"

Failure was not an option.

I took the safety off my M-16 and waited. I hated the thought of what might happen. Every one of my senses was intensely focused. I kept thinking the battalion point man should be approaching shortly and wished they would hurry.

Finally someone came into view. The illumination flares helped me pick out the approaching figure. My finger was on the trigger as he got closer. I didn't know whether to say, "Halt," or call out the name of the point man. If this wasn't an American Marine, I'd be killed.

Once the man got close, I held my breath. My heart was pounding and my trigger finger was tense. I finally called out the Marine's name in a low whisper. If I was wrong and made a move that gave away my location, he could kill me. I was all alone on this side of the ravine.

Even with the light of those flares, the guy looked every bit like a Victor Charlie. Two insect repellent bottles on either side of his helmet made his silhouette look like a coolie hat. His trousers bulged at the pockets so they looked like the wide shorts Charlie usually wore.

Then he called out my name. "Man," he said as he came over, "My heart is racing! Is your safety off?"

"Yes."

"Mine, too."

He'd been thinking just as many what-ifs as I had. They should have put someone taller to walk point that night. A little bit taller Marine would have ensured I didn't mistake him for Victor Charlie. I'll never forget that incident as long as I live.

* * *

The platoons finally crossed the bridge. My fire team was told to fall in behind the company and work our way back up to our section. The darkness made it almost impossible to know who we were with. We were like lost children searching for their mother. After asking just about every person in the column, we finally found a portion of our platoon. We were told to stay put with them for the night; we could find the rest of the platoon when morning came.

As we continued moving, I noticed that some sticks on the ground were glowing. They must have been decaying in a way that made them florescent. I picked up a couple and put them behind my helmet so my fire team would know where I was. Soon all the Marines did the same. It made following someone in the dark a lot easier.

Using resources around me to make life easier was something I learned from my family. We lived in a farming region and our house sat on a hill. It got extremely hot in the summer. In certain places, the ground would split because of the heat. The land was half meadow and half wooded. I liked the quiet and peacefulness of night as well as the clear skies with all those shining stars. We didn't have indoor plumbing, though, and I disliked fetching water and chopping wood.

The only insulation in the house was thick corrugated paper we tacked to the walls and ceiling. The ceiling was made of flank boards. There wasn't even a porch, just a couple of wooden blocks used as steps to two doors that led to the kitchen and the living area. We had an enclosed porch off the back, though, and a door from each room led to the back porch. We bathed there late in the evenings in a galvanized tub.

The interior wasn't decorated at all. We had just a few family photos on the walls and a mirror. There were a couple of throw rugs by the beds and in the kitchen. We lived there for a couple of years, from around 1953 to 1954.

The other house on our property was a small, three-room wooden house allotted to my grandmother and grandfather during the relocation from Florida in the 1830s. Each person was given eighty acres and a home was built for them. The house came with a cast-iron, wood-burning stove with a reservoir on the side where water could be heated.

We also had a handmade dining table with a wooden bench for us kids to sit on. A couple of old rawhide chairs my grandfather made had been passed down as well. A small china cabinet in the kitchen held our dishes, drinking glasses, and coffee cups, none of which matched. The few condiments we had—mustard, catsup, syrup, peanut butter, and salt and pepper—were stored on the dining room table under a dish cloth.

The front room had two double beds in the corners with a couple of small tables for kerosene lamps. During the winter, we rearranged the furniture to get closer to the stove and the heat it put out. The back room was reserved for Mom and Dad.

Their bedroom also served as a storage space. In one corner, Dad placed a long pole across the corner walls. We hung our clothes there after Mom washed and ironed them. There was also a makeshift closet for storing valuable items such as extra clothing and quilts. The quilts were hand-stitched masterpieces. Some were very heavy to keep us warm in winter; others were lightweight for use during summer nights.

Our bathroom was a wooden outhouse several yards behind the house. It had two seats in case someone had an emergency and needed to get in while someone else was there. Although lots of folks used squares of newspaper back then, those were a luxury for us. We rarely got our hands on any. Whenever the Sears and Roebuck catalog came, we were in heaven. We could read it and wish for things at the same time as we used it.

This house had a sheet metal roof that was very rusty. Whenever it rained, the roof leaked. The walls of the house were patched with large sections of cardboard to keep out the worst of the winter. We used everything available to us to make life more comfortable. In Vietnam I did the same to make things a little easier for myself and my fellow Marines.

We were headed up toward Hill 881 to provide reinforcements. By moving at night, we could surprise the enemy. If the battalion needed us, we'd be within striking range or already in position. When we stopped for a few hours, it was so late all I could think about was getting a good night's rest.

My heavy pack served as a good pillow so I leaned back and found a comfortable position. That was the best sleep I ever had in the bush. The next morning we rejoined our platoon. While we waited for further instructions, I dug out some ham slices, crackers, and cheese. Not bad, especially when I had to eat a cold meal.

The fire team and I got along well. I felt relieved that our platoon was the same way. We were a mixed breed of fighting Marines and had every ethnic background imaginable: African American, Hispanic, Native American Indian, and Caucasian. I may have been the only Indian in the platoon but I'm not certain because I didn't go around asking people what nationality they were. I never worried about how I might be treated by the officers or other men. I'd earned the title of Marine and was respected as one.

The only time things seemed strange was a couple of days after arriving at boot camp. After getting our basic supplies, we'd marched over to have our photos taken for our military identification cards. Serial numbers had been assigned to each of us but we didn't know we were supposed to memorize the numbers.

When the photos came out, they were identified only by the serial numbers. All the dark-skinned recruits looked alike because of our bald heads: same skin color, different private. We walked around holding up photos saying things like, "Does this look like me?" Then we'd laugh.

Even though I was the only Native American Indian in the platoon, I still couldn't locate my own photo. I looked like a lot of the Hispanic recruits.

Needless to say, we all went back inside again with new serial numbers. This time, we memorized our serial numbers. If you ask any former Marine young or old, he'll give you his number right off the bat no matter how many years he's been out. Now recruits use their Social Security numbers for their military ID cards so it's a lot easier.

Chapter Ten

A Shau Valley

After morning chow on the mountain, we were told to field clean our M-16s. It didn't take long so we went back to waiting. Since we were out in the bush no one talked loud; when someone spoke, it was in a low monotone voice. We waited and we waited. I got so bored I took a nap until the next command came down.

It seemed we weren't needed to relieve Hill 881, so helicopters picked us up. We moved out of the thickets into an open field to set up 360-degree security for the LZ. I heard the CH-53 Sea Stallions before they appeared over the tree line. The ride was short and we arrived in Phu Bai in no time.

As the Ch-53 landed, we rushed off and assembled away from the landing site. The platoon sergeant said we were going to stay right there for a while. I thought that was kind of strange but I didn't question the leaders. There we sat with all the dirt and debris from the choppers flying around us.

Troops from other units arrived and the platoon sergeant gave us a quick briefing. Our next mission would be in A Shau Valley. No one in the platoon had heard of this place. Someone from the intelligence section said to listen up.

"The A Shau Valley is near the Laotian border," he said while gesturing to a map. "A lot of NVA troops are in the area. The entire place is well fortified. Concrete bunkers manned with heavy automatic weapons sit on both sides of the valley. The troops and supplies are coming through Laos into this country. We need to halt those actions."

This talk went on while the engineers were erecting tents behind us making all kinds of noise. Even though it was getting dark, the briefing continued.

"It's a dangerous mission," the officer said. "The chance that all you Marines will come back out is very slim."

The entire company was surprised. A collective "Ahh" went up; we were shocked. We sat there looking stunned and puzzled.

The platoon sergeant said, "Anyone who wants to go to church services, an announcement will be made later as to the location and time." He asked if we had any questions about the operation.

From what I'd seen on the map, there was nothing to explain. Everything was clear. We had a job to do—go in and stop the heavy traffic of NVA troops and supplies.

Some of the men were upset about the mission, cussing up a storm. I just sat back on my pack and listened to them complain. Soon, they got over being mad.

I really didn't feel like going to chow with the others so I stayed behind and ate C rations. Many other men did the same thing. Several kept talking and talking. Some were short-timers. They said they shouldn't be going on this operation since their wives were expecting them home soon. It seemed like everyone in the tents was talking as it got pretty loud.

Later, church services were held for just about every denomination...Protestant, Catholic, Christian. Someone announced that Protestant services would start in five minutes so I went over. It was a nice service but short; nothing like the lengthy Native American church service I was used to. However, it had a lot of meaning and was a good message for my soul. I thanked the chaplain and walked out feeling better.

As a teenager, I was involved in church activities and singing. One year I was invited to attend a vacation Bible school near my aunt's home. She wanted me to see what the courses were like and to meet people. Since the Indian Baptist Community Church was a few miles from home, my aunt and uncle drove out of their way just to pick me up.

Bible school was an annual thing and lasted about one week. It was taught in English but some of the songs and sermons were in our native language. The school was held at a small white church with a steeple, wooden pews, and an altar but no stained glass.

It seemed like just about every young teenager from the Indian community attended Bible school. Before then, I hadn't realized I had so many cousins in the area. I was flabbergasted at how many people I was related to. My aunt said they were my first, second, third, fourth, and so-on cousins. Once I got over the shock, I was a little disappointed. I thought, "So much for trying to date the pretty girls!"

We studied the Bible, sang songs from the hymn books, and tried to learn the Native American New Testament. We had to learn to read and pronounce the words, which meant trying to say the native alphabet in our own language. The hard part was pronouncing the syllables. Eventually we learned quite a few songs in Creek.

During the first week, we took turns leading the songs. After that, everyone jumped in and sang. We tried very hard not to laugh at each other when we couldn't pronounce the words. We just continued to help each other. After the session ended, a handful of us continued singing and learning our native language. We believed if we didn't learn the language well, it would die out. We wanted to pass it on to future generations.

The Bible school wasn't just about the Native American Bible, either. We also played softball in the pasture behind the church. At times we worked on arts and crafts. After the lessons, I enjoyed listening to sermons, a little in our native language followed by English. The minister was a heavyset Indian with a slight pot belly and a clean-cut appearance. He asked if my group would like to travel with him singing gospel songs in English and our native language.

For the next six years we traveled all over Oklahoma. We visited different Indian communities going from one church to another, singing and praising the good Lord. The younger audiences were amazed at our testimonies and enjoyed our singing. The minister thought that once the young people saw us all dressed up, we would inspire others to return to worship and to learn the native church songs of our ancestors.

Before we sang, we talked about the Bible and its testament and meaning. This really got the people listening. Once we finished performing, the youngest of the audience would come up to greet us on stage. We really had a great following of young men and women who enjoyed the singing and the message. They always asked where we were going to perform next.

After two sessions of singing a night, we headed out to an all-night singing event where people came from all areas to sing. It started as early as 7 p.m. and could run through 7 the next morning. A master of ceremony introduced the groups. Since different singing groups performed throughout the night, everyone got to hear quite a variety of hymns.

My group sang tunes by the Blackwood Brothers Quartet and The Florida Boys, as well as many others. It was an inspirational uplift for me and made a big change in my life. We met a lot of wonderful people; some folks even put us up for the night because they were concerned about us traveling home in the wee hours of the morning. I could only say, "God bless you for your thoughtfulness."

As we all started getting a little older, one member of our group died of natural causes. We found it difficult to go places without his fellowship but we continued even though it was a struggle. We found a piano player and called ourselves The Harmonaires. We continued to travel throughout Oklahoma with the minister and attended as many of the all-night singing events as we could.

So I'd known early on that death comes to us all. In Vietnam, war made death a part of our daily lives. Even back home, though, there were no guarantees anyone would be safe. As Marines, we had to take it all one day at a time, especially this dangerous mission in the A Shau Valley.

Someone mentioned that a Philippine band with young women singers and musicians was playing at the club. I felt kind of bad going to the club right after church but I didn't stay too long. The place was packed and the music was way too loud. Back at the bivouac area some lights were on for what looked like a baseball game.

When I rounded the hardbacks near the gate, I heard a lot of commotion. Troops with the Army Republic of Vietnam (ARVN), also known as the South Vietnamese Army, were staged to the left. The Marines were playing against them in a game of butt-butt. A line of men bent over and locked their heads under the butt of the man in front. Someone from the opposite team ran as fast as he could to jump over the line. It was hilarious.

They did a leg wrestling game, too.

I remember Mom trying to teach us kids that when we were little; she had learned it when she was young. I also remembered the Stick Ball games played during Stomp Dance weekends. Men and women of all ages played that game. Participants used a pair of sticks, each of which had leather netting strung at the end to pick up a stone wrapped in cowhide.

The idea was to see who could hit a carved head of a wooden cow suspended on top of a pole ten or even twenty feet high. In olden times, a real cow skull was hung on top of the pole. In some cases, a wooden fish was used; it just depended on where the game was being held.

About four feet below the cow or fish, a tin can was wrapped around the pole. The object was to score twenty-one points before your opponents could. Striking the head counted as five points. A hit between the head and the tin can earned fewer points, hitting the tin can was worth even less, and so on down the pole. The scorekeeper marked the points on the ground using a long stick. Absolutely no cheating was allowed.

Just about everything else was, though. The game was full contact. Body slams, tackling, and tripping to get the ball away from someone were all allowed. The women had an advantage because they could use their free hand to grab the ball from the men's nets and toss the ball at the cow head.

I tried playing the game once when I was a teenager. I quit because the women got pretty violent wrestling the little ball away from the men. It was a regular free-for-all. Men got their shirts ripped right off in seconds. Some came out bleeding from gouges on their hands and arms. Because serious injuries like broken bones or even death occurred in ancient times, the game's nickname was "the little brother of war." I decided it was just too dangerous.

I watched this game of butt-butt and the leg wrestling for a while. Then I joined a group of Marines sitting around singing songs. You name it, we tried to sing it, from rock & roll to gospel to blues. We were up half the night while the others were still playing with the South Vietnamese troops.

Those troops, dressed in black, were called Black Panthers and were very good fighters, hardcore all the way. I even heard some of them were convicts who'd been let out of prison just to serve in the war. Of course, it was just a rumor, like the "serve jail time or join the military" story some of the recruits spouted in boot camp. All I knew was that they were going to A Shau Valley to support our mission. If they were good fighters, that was all that mattered.

Because of the way I looked, one of the Black Panthers thought I was a Vietnamese national working with the Marines. He patted me on my back and arms saying, "Number one, same, same."

I didn't even try to explain that I was a Native American Indian; I just enjoyed watching them get along with us.

By the time the games were over it was late but the singing kept going. We sounded pretty good on some songs but terrible on others. I guess we got too loud because someone yelled, "Shut up and get some sleep!"

We called it quits. After all, there was no telling what was in store for us the next day. Since I had vowed to take this tour one day at a time, I thanked the good Lord for letting me live one more day.

* * *

The next morning was like any other with the sun coming up over cloudy skies. Marines hacked their morning coughs, and everything was chilly and damp with fog. Some of the men were sleeping on the ground wrapped in their ponchos. I had tried that once but the poncho gathered moisture from body heat. It was okay for some men but not me. I preferred to have my flak jacket over me rather than the poncho.

I got my little stove and heat tabs out to make hot coffee. I planned to sit back and enjoy the morning. One of the Marines told me that while the band had been playing in the club, someone had thrown a CS grenade into the building. The military police had been called in but no one knew who threw it.

By reveille, I finished my first cup of coffee and was working on another with some cocoa and a lot of cream; I'd saved that creamer for weeks. The C-ration creamer packets were usually dried up and difficult to use. If the water got hot enough, though, it dissolved pretty well.

Word came down that formation would be in one hour. We dreaded the information we knew would be passed to us then. Around nine it was getting pretty hot so I made a quick trip to the water buffalo to fill up my canteens. I usually carried a forest-green towel that I wrapped around my neck to keep me cool, so I soaked that while I was over there.

We took our places and waited for the final word. The CH-53s would arrive soon. The formation was short and sweet; our prayers had been answered. We weren't going to A Shau Valley after all. We were going back to Camp Evans and would be assigned other duties. Everyone let out a sigh of relief, including me. It had been a close call.

Although I was relieved, we had a job to do and we would have done it—gone into harm's way—in an instant. But another day to fight would come soon enough.

* * *

We were not happy; we had all those extra C rations and ammunition but no place to go. Still, I felt the good Lord was watching over me. The CH-53s came in later. Before we knew it, we were landing.

This was my second time coming back to Camp Evans. It seemed like each time I came back, the area had changed just a little. More and more troops were coming in as the war continued. The base always seemed busier and there were more tents set up every time.

The administration clerk directed us to our new company area. We dropped our gear on some cots and waited for the next assignment. I always took advantage of these breaks by squeezing in five- to ten-minute power naps. They kept me from being tired the rest of the day. One thing I learned fast was to always take advantage of any little time I could to eat or nap. The rest, I knew, would take care of itself.

Chapter Eleven
Security Detail

The company decided to rest us for a couple of days. Earlier that week my squad had been tasked to provide security detail for the Engineering Water Section. Two water trucks had to leave the compound to tank up at the river near a local village. They would make multiple trips until the camp's supply was full again.

We headed up to the Battalion S-4. It wasn't long before the trucks arrived, stirring up a trail of dust. The reddish cloud swirled around us as they came to a squelching stop. One of the trucks had a bladder in the back, another was a water tanker, and the third was a six-by.

The six-by was a basic truck used to transport troops and supplies. Some were olive drab in color and some were camouflaged. They burned diesel and sat high on huge tires. Although the beds of stateside trucks might be covered, in Vietnam they were open. It could carry about twenty troops if men sat on the benches and the truck bed.

We climbed aboard and proceeded down the dirt road out of Camp Evans, leaving a trail of blowing dust. The sun was hot, and the sky was a clear blue with no clouds in sight. The low water area where we filled up looked like a washed-out road. There weren't any bridges nearby and the road was a mess from the currents.

Once the six-by was empty, it left. The water trucks backed up to the edge of the river and the men got the hoses ready to pump. Since this would be an all-day affair, we were told to take chow. The day was going to be a scorcher and there was no way to prepare for the heat. All I could do was wet down my towel and wrap it around my neck. Sometimes I held up both ends to provide a little shade.

We had no sunglasses or sunscreen in our gear. We had to live with the conditions, just like when I was a kid in Oklahoma. When I was around ten years old, sometime in the mid-1950s, the summers were very hot. We had no air conditioning or refrigerator. Only the shade kept us cool.

Somehow Dad always managed to have ice available. We kept it in galvanized buckets. It was so nice to have ice water on those hot days, like tasting a little piece of heaven. I still remember hot nights when my aunt, uncle, and parents sat on the front porch of the Big House in the late evening telling stories. Many of the tales were about things that happened in the "good old days."

My Dad chewed a tobacco called Day's Work. Back in those days women were also known to have chewed tobacco, smoked pipes, and even dipped snuff. During those storytelling sessions, the sound of spitting would be followed by a loud splat hitting the ground somewhere in the darkness. If you weren't careful and happened to get in the way, it was easy to end up being spit on.

Some of the stories they told had been handed down from my grandparents. A few of those were very scary. All the kids ended up sitting close to our parents for those. To make matters worse, the dogs would start barking for no reason, which made us jump and shake. All we knew was that something was out there in the dark, which was pitch black. It scared us out of our wits.

The story telling went on into the wee hours of the night with folks chewing tobacco, smoking their hand-rolled cigarettes and pipes, and drinking ice-cold glasses of water with no worries. For times like this, Dad invested in large, galvanized water can with a lid so the ice would last a little longer. The cooler even had a spout at the front. Mom always made plenty of iced tea and cherry or strawberry Kool-Aid. I believe a package of Kool-Aid sold for a nickel. It was a quick way to beat the heat.

That day in Vietnam, there wasn't an ice cube in sight. We patrolled both sides of the river around the watering area to make sure there were no booby traps or landmines. A lot of villagers were fetching water and some set up little shops along the road. I believe the route was Highway One, which ran north-south. I didn't know if it ran into North Vietnam or not, and at that moment, I didn't care. I wasn't planning on going that far.

The duty was simple. The trucks made several trips while we maintained security. We had nothing but time. I sat and watched the villagers. One old woman started a fire; she had a little black kettle and some aluminum pots and pans beside her with a skinned duck. She put the whole duck in the kettle along with some green onions. As she worked, kids gathered around her.

Meat was a pretty unusual thing for the villagers to have. It was too expensive and spoiled quickly in the heat. Often they ate seafood, eels, frog's eggs, and occasionally duck, chicken, or pork. Mostly they ate the vegetables they grew like yams, onions, and bamboo shoots as well as the bananas, coconuts, and other fruits.

Back home, my family had also used what they could off the land. To supplement the canned goods during the lean winter months, my older brother and other relatives went rabbit hunting. They'd wait for a heavy snow then go hunting. They usually came back with at least four rabbits.

We hunted cottontails, and each adult rabbit weighed about one to one and a half pounds. When served with another dish, we could feed a family of four with one rabbit. After one of the boys cleaned them,

Mom cut the rabbits up, coated the pieces with milk and seasoned flour then dropped them into hot grease until they turned golden brown. When it was ready, no one could tell if it was chicken or rabbit.

To go along with our wild meal, Mom served pinto beans, rice, fried potatoes, and lots of hot sourdough biscuits. Sometimes she made sourdough cornbread. Our beverages were a choice of coffee, hot tea or a glass of water. That was a feast. That old woman cooking her duck must have been looking forward to a similar feast. Judging from the number of children she attracted, the kids looked forward to the feast as well.

The vendors were selling American cigarettes and booze, of course, but most of them sold food. One had sweetened rice cakes, boiled rice made into patties with sugar. She also had some homemade candies. Since rice was the main staple for the Vietnamese people, they made it into everything from stir fry to noodles.

The rest of the low river crossing area was pretty busy. Lots of other activity took place on both sides of the river. Women did their laundry and villagers hauled water in large square tins that dangled from their poles. It looked easy; they had a rhythm and as they swung their arms, the pole bounced up and down.

I thought, "I can do that."

I did stuff like that all my younger years. After school, we changed out of our school clothes into our old, work clothes. We chopped wood, split the wood into kindling, and gathered wood chips to start the morning fire. Dad split and stacked the larger logs for us to carry into the house. Once that was done, we fetched water for cooking and washing dishes.

The water came from a nearby house that belonged to my Uncle John. He and his family had moved to the city and seldom visited. The house had well water drawn with a hand pump. We thought it was neat to use the muscles in our arms to pump the water. It tasted great and always stayed cool.

We filled small and large buckets to carry back to our house. The distance was about the length of a football field. It wasn't easy and we usually spilled half the water by the time we got inside. When we wanted to bathe, it took a lot of extra work to fill the galvanized tubs. As we went back and forth, large dishpans atop the stove warmed the water for our baths.

I worked hard as a kid and as a man was even stronger. Being a good American, I wanted to do something for the Vietnamese people. I thought I'd help a few carry their water. It would be a nice gesture and would pass the time a little faster.

Was I wrong! The long pole dug into my shoulder muscle and almost damaged me. Plus, I couldn't get that rhythm going. I walked just a few yards and had to stop. They all laughed at me, especially the kids. They all thought I was Vietnamese and had forgotten how to carry water.

I went back to watching the villagers pretty quick. I didn't mind. I was curious about how they lived, their customs, and their culture. The Vietnamese were interesting and reminded me of my own culture. Their ceremonies and services were similar; they lived off the land; and even their facial features, especially the ones with high cheekbones, seemed familiar.

The beautiful young ladies were dressed in white ao dais. Even though they appeared not to wear makeup, they truly were gorgeous.

I noticed that the older women had black teeth. When I asked one of the kids why, they said it was from chewing beetle nut gum. It relaxed them but their teeth turned black after years of chewing it. A kid showed me the old woman's raw beetle nut; it looked like a raw acorn.

I had to be extremely cautious around the kids. I'd heard they would try to get to the grenades and pull the pin while it was still on you. I sure didn't want that to happen. Some of the Marines gave them candy from their C rations so I did too. It wasn't much but they sure did go for it.

When the old woman added some rice to her black kettle, it smelled great. By the time the trucks returned from their first trip, it was really hot. None of us had any shade and the driver was already pretty dirty. I wondered if he always worked back in the rear. I also thought he could have stayed at least a little clean since he worked with water.

Despite the heat, time actually went by faster than I thought. There was never a dull moment at the low water crossing. Cars and small buses heading both directions carried people who were all dressed up. They waved as they drove by. Around noon I dug into my pack hoping to find some ham slices but had no luck. However, I found a ham and egg loaf, which would have been okay if I had hot sauce but I was out of that, too. But I ate it anyway.

The kids sat there and talked to me. Just like the ARVN troops, the kids thought I was a Vietnamese hired by the Marine Corps as a scout or something. They kept saying, "You number one" and "Same, same." They would point to my skin and then to their own arms.

I told them I was Indian but they didn't know what the word meant. I even put my hand over my mouth and patted it to make the "Hollywood Indian sounds" but they still didn't understand. Eventually, I told them they had to move. They did without any hassle. Maybe they were showing me respect since we looked alike. I remember thinking they were typical curious kids, just like American kids.

Sometime after the trucks left for their second trip, I soaked my green towel again and draped it over my head. Finally, the trucks barreled back down the road kicking up dust. The driver hollered that they were finished. It must have been more than 100 degrees as we returned to Camp Evans.

The hot wind hit us in the face while the driver raced down the highway shifting gears now and then. It reminded me of the times I hauled hay with my Dad. Although he pretty much did whatever job he could find, hauling hay was his bread and butter. In fact, it might have been his favorite thing to do. He acted like it was as much a hobby as a job. It certainly gave him a chance to show off his skills and his strength.

He'd toss those hefty hay bales up on the truck without a problem. The bales were usually stacked at least four layers high to cut down on the number of trips the truck had to make. He could stack those bales so they wouldn't fall off even without ropes to tie them down. It was like an art form for him. Whenever we worked alongside him, he also made our jobs easier.

Those days usually started when someone came to the house to get him. He never hesitated. He would change into his work clothes, grab his heavy leather gloves, put on his brown brimmed hat, and head out the door. The rancher offered him some chewing tobacco and Dad climbed into the truck. We never knew where he was going. He would either be in the field loading the hay or stacking the hay from truck to barn.

Hay hauling was backbreaking with lots of dust and hay particles flying around. It got all over our clothes, in our hair, and up our noses. Dad was covered in dust and hay particles the whole day, chewing and spitting tobacco as he worked and periodically grabbing ice water from the galvanized water can.

I often wondered how Dad managed to work on those hot days hauling hay. At times I'd wished we were rich so Dad wouldn't have to do all that hard labor for such long hours in the heat. But that was life and survival for him; sometimes I think he enjoyed it more than anything. I really can't say. He was quiet and kept things to himself but he always, always provided for the family. That's what mattered most to him.

After we'd unloaded the hay truck, the driver would tear down the highway. All the loose hay would blow around the bed and hit us in the face. The wind blowing the hay off your body felt good but the heat of the wind was miserable.

In Vietnam, that Marine drove the same way as he took us back to camp...fast and faster. We were dirty and covered in dust by then, and the wind felt good yet the heat was miserable. It was amazing that the experience was so similar even though I was in such a different environment.

Of course, I'd rather go too fast than too slow. Besides, with the risk of ambush or attack at slower speeds, it probably would have been even more uncomfortable at a slower pace in that heat. I knew that from when I'd been a kid and had ridden with my uncle.

My uncle had been the quiet type with sleepy eyes. He was short and pot-bellied, and always wore a white shirt and an old brown fedora...even while chopping wood. He was the type of person who had no enemies, and there wasn't one streak of meanness in him. I never heard bad words from his mouth nor did I ever see him angry.

My cousins always teased him and his sons harassed him because he drove very, very slowly. One time when we all got dressed up to go to town, we piled into the car while he let the engine warm up. After about ten minutes, we were off. I believe he was going every bit of thirty miles an hour on the highway.

It was very hot that day and heat poured in through the open windows. Everyone zoomed by us honking because he was moving so slowly. It didn't bother him one bit. His boys told him to speed it up because everyone who'd passed us was already returning from town. They used to joke and imitate his driving but he was a wonderful man and uncle.

Back at camp, the security team got the privilege of using the showers first and ahead of the designated time. We got out of our dirty jungle clothes right away. I followed the others wearing only a fresh towel and my jungle boots with no socks. What a sight I was. My arms were brown and certain parts of my body were white; the others guys were the same.

The showers were so nice, especially on such a hot day. We couldn't stay in long, just enough to soap up, rinse off, and then leave. Even though it was fast, I felt much better and put on clean clothes.

The Marines who'd joined the company with me paid me a visit. Since we hadn't seen each other in quite a while, we exchanged stories about our platoons and what we'd done. I asked if anyone received mail from home. I hadn't received any yet, but I wrote my folks some so I hoped a few letters would come soon. Mail took about six weeks to start, so we just had to be patient.

The letters I wrote home were always full of descriptions. I'd started doing that back in boot camp, especially after we got to Camp Pendleton in California. All the recruits were stunned by that place. From a distance the buildings looked new, and we thought it was a huge resort with all those tall palm trees and orange bird of paradise blooms neatly lined up near the walkways.

The blue Pacific Ocean was visible from the bus. As we drove in that first day, I thought, "What a beautiful sight."

I watched the waters and the waves with whitecaps running near the shore. As we got closer, I could watch the whitecaps melt away as they hit the sand.

Even the inside of the barracks was impressive. The floors were very shiny, not like at MCRD where most of our training had been held. The beds looked new, were solid, and had thick mattresses, also unlike the bunks at MCRD.

Once the DI dropped off our platoon, someone went looking for the head. Next thing we knew he yelled for us to come and look at the white shining urinals against the wall, white sinks, and clean, tiled showers. We were going to like Camp Pendleton.

That first afternoon, I wrote home to tell my folks I was starting Primary Marksmanship Instruction (PMI). I really poured it on thick for them. I told them how beautiful the ocean was and that I could see the mountains to the northeast. I also mentioned how the ocean breeze smelled...fresh and clean, and that it cleared out our lungs when we ran around Edison Range.

Well, I couldn't say that Vietnam had any cool, salty breezes or snazzy barracks. Instead I told them about the people working in the fields or about the things I saw whenever we moved through their villages. There were so many new things to see, so my letters home always had something different to tell.

Chapter Twelve
Recon Hill

One of the Marines who came in with us hadn't been drinking enough water and got heat exhaustion. He'd been medevacked out of the bush. Another time, the same Marine didn't purify his water and came down with diarrhea so bad he became dehydrated. Since helicopters couldn't land in the dense vegetation in the mountain, there was no medevac. He'd had to sweat it out in the bush.

The medevac runs made by those pilots were something else. Those men who flew into the mountains to retrieve Marines, even for dehydration, made some daring flights to get our troops out of the jungle. I was glad they were on our side.

They said the Marine was taking it easy on his cot since he needed his beauty sleep. We all laughed and agreed we were lucky not to have gotten diarrhea yet. We joked that as long as we had our ham and lima beans, we'd be all right. We also laughed about the Marines who got drunk on two or three cans of beer; we thought it hilarious how they talked trash.

All my brothers were sticking with the sodas like me.

As a group, we decided to call to ourselves The Magnificent Seven, and we got together again not long after that first meeting.

Back at the platoon, it was mail call. Some men acted all wild and crazy, as if they were running to see a naked woman. We were still new at that point so we didn't understand how important mail call was to those who'd been there a while. Mail was the most important thing; it helped morale. I remember how the faces of so many troops looked when their names were called out.

"I wrote a letter on a C-ration box top," one guy said. "I wrote 'free' in the corner where the stamp normally goes. They delivered it!"

"I've been using stamps on my letters," I said.

"We don't have to put stamps on our mail. We're in a war zone."

"I've been writing air mail under the stamp," I said.

The whole group got a big laugh about that.

We usually stayed up late talking. Those were special moments. It was like talking among brothers. One Marine said his folks were going to send a package of goodies and that he'd share with us. Someone else said he would share his first letter.

"Hey," we said right away, "we don't want to hear anything gross and mushy!"

"Yeah," one guy laughed, "we'll just smell the envelope."

It was fun, too, with men making jokes. Many would pass a letter back and say, "Why is my girlfriend writing you?" or "Who do you know who can read or write?"

As for those letters with perfume on them, I believe everyone took a sniff as they went from hand to hand. I can still smell the fragrances from some of those letters.

At those times, my mind usually drifted back home. I'm sure everyone else was thinking the same. Since I didn't have a wife or girlfriend, I didn't have to worry about some of the things the married men did. I wondered if Mom knew I was in Vietnam or if she knew anything about the war. I wasn't sure because she didn't watch the news at all.

I often wondered if she and Dad were okay and thought about the family get-togethers that happened almost monthly. We always had a dinner to celebrate birthdays and the family would celebrate together. My Mom and sisters would fix a big spread. I could close my eyes and see all that food on the dinner table: homemade meatloaf, chicken and dumplings, golden fried chicken, mashed potatoes, sourdough cornbread, and much more.

Mom usually made the desserts. One of her best was banana pudding. She also made lemon meringue pie, mincemeat pie, pecan pie, and German chocolate cake with coconut and topped with vanilla ice cream. Just thinking about all those foods made me hungry.

I left mail call and dug through my pack to see what I could snack on. I found some beans and wieners, which I had held on to for some time, as well as hot sauce from our last re-supply. I got out my John Wayne, the tiny P-38 can opener the actor had demonstrated in a training film, and had a quick meal. It wasn't the best snack but it had to do under the circumstances.

The guys showed up after mail call with some good news. We all got letters from home. We had a lot to talk about and were a happy bunch of Marines. The stories we shared gave us comfort and made us feel secure with each other. We joked about each other's news. The laughter definitely helped keep us from going crazy, knowing we had much more time left in country.

I believe we saw each other a few more times, always after mail call, before our platoons were sent in different directions. Every so often, we would see each other on an operation and gave each other the high-five or thumbs-up. It was always great to see them and know they were still safe even out in the bush. If our platoons stopped long enough, we brought each other up to date.

Other times we talked about the leeches sucking the blood out of our legs and how miserable we were. Once a leech crawled between my legs but I couldn't feel it because my trousers were wet. Later I had some pain in that area so I reached down, felt something lumpy, and pulled at it thinking it was a tick. When it wouldn't budge, I realized it was a leech. Whew!

Marching through all that jungle meant being bitten by ants, ticks, leeches, and bugs I didn't know the names of. That was familiar, too. As a kid, whenever I walked the couple of miles to school, I took a gravel road. If I was running late I'd cut through the pasture and woods. In warmer months, snakes hid in the bushes and along the trail. Plus, cockle burrs stuck to your socks and clothing.

Even worse were those pesky chiggers or no-see-ums. If you've never been bitten by one, you're lucky. Those little insects would eat me alive and leave little red marks that made me itch all over. Their bites lasted many days and made life miserable. And you sure as heck didn't want them in the wrong place, like between your legs.

At least I could see the leeches and do something about them. One Marine told me to squirt insect repellent on the leeches and they'd fall right off. I'd been using a cigarette to burn them off. That is the only time I used the cigarettes in Vietnam—to burn leeches off my body.

* * *

After a couple of weeks in the bush on an operation, we headed back to Camp Evans again. We knew the routine—secure an area for the choppers, set up security for the LZ, and sit down to wait. For once, I was looking forward to going back to camp. I wanted to see if any more mail had come.

After chow came a mail call. We gathered around as they passed out the envelopes and packages. I got really lucky and received three letters. I usually reread all my letters in case I missed something the first time, and I always opened the important ones, like those from

Mom, first. Some girls I'd met during the six months prior to shipping out also wrote.

Following mail call, the platoon sergeant briefed us on our next mission. We were headed to a mountaintop for thirty days to provide security for the Recon Radio Relay Team. I'd been in country almost three months, and I thought my time was going pretty fast.

Yes, I was counting the days. I'd never thought I would do that. This assignment would be great as long as we didn't have to march around those slopes. We all thought it would be a good break, like a little R&R in a mountain retreat.

* * *

We left around the first of June 1967. I gathered what I needed for thirty days: letter-writing gear, extra clothes and especially socks, a soft cover for my helmet, C rations, and plenty of ammo. We were loaded down but we all felt we'd rather be overburdened with war gear than be sorry.

Our mission was simple: provide security for the Recon Relay Team on the mountain. The radio team had communication equipment that monitored the reconnaissance units patrolling the bush. If the units needed support, they relayed the transmissions through the team on the mountaintop.

The Marines in my fire team were reassigned and I was given two new men. Both were fresh from the states. One was Hispanic from Corpus Christi, Texas. He had a small build but he talked enough for two guys. The other troop was an African American from Detroit. He was skinny and I soon learned that he clowned around a lot.

Since they'd probably gone through the same thing I had upon arrival in Vietnam, I wanted them to feel comfortable. When I introduced myself, they called me "Sir." I started laughing right away. I wasn't laughing at them, not really. But it was just like graduation day at boot camp in MCRD.

All the privates who graduated that day had base liberty so we roamed around checking out areas we hadn't seen during training. Some of the Marines headed right over to the Enlisted Club. I stopped by and was amazed. It looked like a high-class club in the movies. The place was packed with Marines and their lady guests and parents.

I left as quickly as I'd entered. I wished I could have paid my parents' travel costs so they could have been with me that day. Still, it was nice to see everyone else's family and to know that everyone had accomplished something important.

Later that day, things got kind of funny. We never knew if the Marine coming toward us was an officer or not, so we saluted. It would be just our luck that if we didn't salute, it would be an officer. The last thing we wanted was to be chewed out in front of all those guests. We wound up saluting each other smartly then laughing.

In Vietnam, we didn't wear any insignia because Charlie liked to snipe at high-ranking Marines. That meant these new recruits had no way of knowing if I was an officer. Just like in boot camp, when in doubt, these guys had saluted.

"I'm only a corporal," I said. "You don't have to call me sir."

I entered their emergency information in my little green book. All fire team leaders were required to have a book with up-to-date emergency information for their Marines. In the event of medical evacuation or other problems, I'd know who to contact.

As we boarded the CH-46, I thought this might be our easiest assignment yet. I wished all the operations in the bush could be like this one. My tour of duty would be safe and my time would be over before I knew it. Of course, things are never what you wish them to be.

As the chopper took off, the spirit of the men seemed happy. Everyone was looking forward to our thirty-day assignment at the top of the mountain. I wondered what else we'd do besides providing security. No one had said anything about running patrols or ambushes. I wondered if we were only going to pull bunker or hole watch?

The LZ was a small area at the top of the mountain. It was a pretty hairy situation for the pilot. The helicopter couldn't touch the ground so we had to jump off with our gear and roll away as the chopper swayed back and forth.

As usual, we fought blowing wind, dust, and debris from the choppers. Once the choppers took off, the platoon guide took each fire team to a specific location and told us to stay there unless instructed otherwise. My team's position faced Camp Evans and the coast, so we had a great view of the valley.

Right below our position was a string of barbed wire with lots of cans hanging from it. If anyone touched the wire, the cans would make enough racket to alert us. It didn't look like we had enough wire in front of our position, though. When I mentioned that to the platoon guide, he said a claymore mine should take care of it.

The claymore was known as the anti-personnel mine M18A1 and was a directional fixed fragmentation mine. Our team used it in defensive positions in the event we were attacked by mass VC troops. When detonated, it shot a large number of steel fragments in a fan-shaped zone a couple meters high and probably fifty meters wide. Its range depended on how it was set up but normally could reach thirty to fifty meters.

I told the team to make sure the mine faced away from us so we didn't get killed. They laughed as they started down the mountain. After setting the mine, they indicated that the whole area around our bunker was steep. We were ready for our watch now. It was such a nice view we hoped nothing happened.

* * *

Mornings on the mountain started out cool but got hot and humid as the day progressed. From our fighting holes, we had a spectacular 360-degree panoramic view. The South China Seas were to our front, small mountains with lush vegetation sat on our left, and behind us in the distance were more mountains. Between the mountains, a valley wound through the jungles.

The valley headed toward Laos. I could barely make out the treetops off in the distance. The radio relay team let me look through their powerful VC scope. It magnified everything so well; I could periodically spot movement in the valley. I had no way of knowing whether it was Charlie or farmers. Only the radio team knew for sure.

Our protection included a 106-mm recoilless (RCL) rifle with its own specialty team, a couple of tubes of 81-mm mortars, and a .50-caliber machine gun. The RCL was self-propelled and mostly used for defense. The mortars were black tubes about four feet tall. Each sat on a tripod base plate at an angle.

This fire support was for the recon units out in the bush. Our daily activity consisted of cleaning our M-16s and writing letters. Each of us was given a five-gallon water container and a case of C rations. They also gave us some onions and hot sauce to spice up the food.

Days weren't bad. The nights, though, were like horror stories. The area was surrounded by large rocks. When darkness fell, from those rocks came swarms of the largest rats I'd ever seen. Some were as large as opossums. They overran us, poking around for the smallest crumb.

When one jumped across my chest one night, I assumed it was a baby because it was so small. What spooked me most was all the noise they made. We heard them rummaging through the trash, rattling the empty cans for any morsel of food, and making weird squeaking sounds. Loud, weird squeaking sounds. I didn't want to get bitten so I became a very light sleeper even when I was dog-tired.

The rats came almost every night. No one really got a good night's sleep the entire time. Most of us napped during the day just to get some rest. Prior to having my first encounter with the rodents, I slept by myself away from my team. After the rat incident, I joined them. They had set up a wide area where we could spread out. We took turns standing hole watch while the others slept or kept the rats away.

During this thirty-day duty my team grew pretty close, especially the Hispanic Marine and me. We talked about our lives like a little brother talking to a big brother. This Marine kept saying he wanted me to come to Corpus Christi so he could show me around.

One afternoon, Corpus and I were talking. The other Marine from Detroit was sitting on the sandbags. When we looked over, he had his trousers pulled down and was holding his private parts and checking them out. It looked like he was playing with himself so I asked him what he was doing.

"I can't believe you're playing with yourself in front of us," Corpus joked.

Detroit laughed. "No, man, I'm not playing with myself. Something's wrong down there. It looks like a tick."

"Pull up your trousers," I said, "And go see the corpsman."

"I can't believe that," Corpus muttered as Detroit left. "What a weirdo."

We both thought he was a little strange but we got a good laugh.

Chapter Thirteen
Phantoms and B-52s

The first two weeks or so on the mountain were just fine. One day, I was tasked to take a small group on a recon mission. They told me to pick my men, so I walked around the platoon perimeter and selected some pretty good volunteers...if you want to call it volunteering.

Five Marines were assigned with me, and we were given a PRC-25 radio. I made sure we were on the same frequency as the rest of the company and that we had the correct call signs. We were cleared through the company and battalion radio operators and went over our checkpoints on the map.

The mission called for us to go some meters from the camp on a finger of land extending off the mountainside. I gathered everyone together and we checked to make sure we had our soft covers, cartridge belts with two full canteens, and our M-16s with several rounds of ammunition in the magazines. We eliminated any rattling from our equipment and put on our war paint. After an hour, we were ready to leave.

I double-checked to make sure the 81-mm mortar section had our checkpoints plotted in case we needed fire support. Finally we stepped through the fence line by weaving in and out of the barbed wire. As we worked our way down the mountain, I turned and looked back up. It was very steep but it didn't feel that steep walking down.

As we moved into a dense thicket, all the noise from the mountaintop faded. We were on our own. We tried to walk softly and not step on anything that would make noise as we moved through the dark, damp undergrowth. I was proud of this recon team; everyone was doing a good job.

Periodically we stopped to listen. The jungle was so quiet; the only sounds came from insects. No birds chirped. When we stopped to listen again, a strange noise floated through the trees. We stood extremely still for quite some time trying to figure out what the noise was and where it was coming from. It might have been Mr. Charles sneaking up on us using the same technique we were using—walk, stop, listen.

Finally we saw what was making the noise. It was a huge black centipede—eighteen to twenty inches long and a good two inches wide. The sound of all its feet moving through the leaves was loud enough to sound like a person creeping through the jungle. We continued forward wondering what we would run into next.

The point man walked up to a tree limb. As I reached out to support myself, he pointed to a green viper covered with leaves. It appeared ready to strike. If I had touched the limb, I probably would have been bitten. The team went around it, which put us off our path, but I didn't want to take any chances. It could have been the bamboo viper we'd been warned about; they were the most deadly.

As we continued deeper into the forest, we heard something like a person chopping wood. The sound came from deep within the jungle. As we moved toward it, we saw smoke coming through the canopy in the valley below. It couldn't be farmers because we were too far into the mountains. We whispered that we'd probably located a Vietnamese whiskey still since it was so far from any village.

I radioed this information to the platoon and the company. They wanted us to see if we could move closer and identify who might be there but the bush was too thick. Although we could hear talking and shouting in Vietnamese, we couldn't see a thing. We turned around and started back, being extra careful to stay away from the snake, laughing softly even as we did.

We didn't have to stop and listen on the way back so it didn't take long to reach the perimeter. Before I released the men, I said they did a great job and patted each of them on the back. I then briefed the platoon sergeant and the radio team about what we'd seen, what we'd heard, and the direction the noise had come from.

My fire team wanted to know all about the patrol so I talked while fixing something to eat. I found a can of ham and lima beans, added hot sauce and cheddar cheese, and heated it up. One of the men asked about the direction the noise had come from in relation to our position. He put some extra cans on the barbed wire strung in that direction.

The next day we watched a close air support strike on the opposite side of the valley. The jets screamed above us; those F-4 Phantom jets truly were a beautiful sight as they flew down into the valley. The Phantom was silver with a two-man crew. It carried from 10,000 to 16,000 pounds of weapons and came in at about 1,400 knots. Most often they were equipped with napalms, bombs filled with petroleum and chemical thickeners.

As they thundered by, the pilot in one of the cockpits was almost visible as it screamed right passed us. Then they dropped bombs with high explosive ordinance. Next, they dropped napalms with their bright orange glow and thick black clouds of smoke.

For at least thirty minutes, the jets dropped loads again and again. Whoever was down there didn't have a chance. That was our entertainment for the day. All we could do was watch and say "ooh" and "aah."

The next morning we were in for another surprise. More jets were called in. We heard them high above but they didn't come down. Instead, a couple of UH-1B Huey gunships fired rockets at a target. It was very early and the valley was still heavy with fog and mist. The Huey's twin machine guns blazed away as the rockets launched.

After the area had been peppered with the Huey's entire ordinance, a CH-53 flew in very fast and landed just long enough to extract some men from the valley floor. They were recon Marines who'd been surrounded the day before. They spent the night trying to work their way out but got pinned down again.

Victor Charlie fired everything he had as the chopper took off; it looked like Christmas lights blinking in the darkness. Green tracer rounds flew everywhere and red tracers were fired at the chopper from several areas. Those men had been absolutely surrounded. Without assistance, they never would have gotten out.

The enemy's small-arms fire didn't last long. The F-4 Phantoms came in with the first napalm. There was a burst of yellow and orange with black smoke encircling the blast. Then the glow shot out to engulf and suffocate everything in its path. Next came high explosive ordinance shrapnel that knocked down trees like they were twigs.

After a couple more bomb runs, the Phantoms left as quickly as they arrived. We stood on the mountaintop and applauded the action. What teamwork! They'd rescued the recon team then put a lot of hurt on the enemy. It was like clockwork. Strong Marine Corps training helped the unit prevail.

After the show, we fortified our defensive position in case we were probed that night by the VC. We also wanted to be ready if they decided to hit us with Bangalore torpedoes. I never saw a Bangalore torpedo except in training but the VC used them all the time. The Bangalore was designed to clear a path through barbed wire, and could be used to clear mine-fields as well.

I kind of doubted they would use those on the steep mountain but I wasn't for sure. There was also the chance they'd throw satchel charges at bunkers or fighting holes. The satchel charge was nothing more than a block of explosions with a TNT composition inside a canvas bag. They were easy to make but were as deadly as any high-tech weapon.

That night, we were at heightened alert until we were told to stand down. That meant 100 percent alert followed by 50 percent later. One man would sleep while the other stayed awake. Since my team had three men, we divided the watch three ways.

No infiltrators showed up that night but we saw a few pop-up illumination flares on the opposite side of the mountains. Some folks were getting edgy so the 81-mm mortar section put out some flares as well. We heard the canisters soar up into the night then saw their small parachutes float down.

Those 81-mm flares put out a lot of light; each burned with an intensity equivalent to 50,000 candle power but only lasted a minute or so. That was fine with me. It lit up the area enough so we could see down the mountainside. The next morning we were still at heightened alert at 50 percent status.

Just another day in Vietnam.

* * *

All of our time wasn't spent sitting around or sleeping or cleaning our rifles; we received Marine Corps training on topics such as maps, compasses, calling for close air support, calling for artillery fire support, and, of course, sanitation and hygiene. Navy corpsman gave classes on the last two subjects.

At one point, we also fired our M-16s off the mountainside to ensure they were in working condition. That also allowed us to use up the old ammunition we'd carried in our magazines for so many months. We then replaced them with new 5.56-mm rounds and were ready for anything.

I was getting to know my men pretty well, and we really trusted each other. What we said to each other stayed only with us. I still remember the personal talks we had, especially between me and the young Marine from Corpus Christi.

"I had a crush on my high school teacher," he told me. "She's gorgeous, and she loves me, too. I'd had some feelings for her and really liked her but didn't show it. I didn't want anyone to know, especially the other students. It always made me feel good when she called me by name in class, though."

"That's puppy love," I said. "Everybody falls in love with their teacher."

"No. This is for real!"

"I'd have to see it to believe it."

"I'll make you a deal," he said. "As soon as we're back in the States, you visit me. I'll introduce you to her."

I told him about one of my teachers who always dressed very nice. "I could always smell her perfume a mile away," I said, "but I wasn't in love with her."

"I always knew when she was in the area by the fragrance she left behind; it smelled wonderfully sexy." We both started laughing and wondered why older women always looked sexy to us but the younger girls didn't have any appeal.

It's funny, too, that a woman's perfume was one of my strongest memories from the day I enlisted. The thought of joining the military had come up once before and I'd talked to my brother about it. When it came up a second time, it was even more tempting.

During the Christmas holiday, I decided to join. I didn't tell anyone in my family what I was going to do. I didn't care what they thought. At the time, I was a slender kid about 6 feet tall and weighed 150 pounds. I had thick black hair neatly combed in the old slick back ducktail style. I wore Levis, western boots, and always had on a solid blue shirt.

I asked my brother to give me a nice haircut so I would look sharp for the recruiters. I planned to go to the federal building and speak to a recruiter that Monday. My brother cautioned me to think twice. At the time, I knew nothing about the war in Vietnam or anything else happening in the world. I hardly watched the news on television much less read the newspaper.

I was looking forward to joining the military. I was twenty years old and looking for adventure. Nothing was happening in Konawa. I needed to learn a trade and I wanted to get away from Oklahoma. Fishing and hunting on weekends got old pretty quick. My plan was to go up to the recruiting station and find out what the different branches of service had to offer.

The federal building was a typical government structure, a long rectangle of large cement blocks. There were marble accents in front and in the foyer. I entered from the side and found the floor to be very shiny. It housed most of the usual agencies like the FBI, Social Security Administration, IRS, and the recruiters.

I walked straight to the Air Force recruiter's office. Someone in the next office said he'd stepped out and would be back shortly. They told me to have a seat if I wanted. I picked up a brochure and glanced at the programs the Air Force offered. After about thirty minutes and still no recruiter, I left.

A couple of young ladies were getting out of the elevator. When I stepped inside, I could smell their perfume. Humming a tune, I pushed a button thinking I'd go home. As I headed for the exit a young Marine gunnery sergeant asked me where I was headed. He wanted to know why I'd chosen the Air Force then asked me to come to his office to see what the Marine Corps could offer.

I didn't think it would hurt to listen so I went to his office. When we caught the elevator, that same perfume still lingered. In his office, he handed me a catalog to see if anything caught my eye. He explained how a program works in the military—not just the Marine Corps but all branches. He could sign me up but it was it was up to me to pass the tests. If I failed, I would be placed someplace else.

"Okay," I said, "let me see what the Marine Corps can do for me."

"How many years?" he asked.

"Four."

He looked surprised and I said, "My brother served three years before being discharged honorably. I want to go one better than him."

He completed the contract and I signed. He had to conduct a background check and request a copy of my birth certificate from the Department of Public Health in Oklahoma City, so I could leave for a few hours. He gave me a token to get something to eat at one of the diners. I took the elevator back to the lobby then shot out of the building.

When the fresh air hit me, I stood there on the steps wondering, "What did I just do?"

A year and a half later I was on top of a mountain half a world away. The only perfume I smelled came on other men's letters at mail call. But I'd gotten what I'd wanted: job skills, adventure, and a whole lot of new experiences.

* * *

Two corpsmen were assigned to us on the mountaintop. I thought both of them were weird but they were great corpsmen. They took photographs of each other sitting on a homemade toilet they'd made out of the sleeve of a C-ration box. They snapped photos like they were tourists on a new adventure. They were also somewhat exposed in the pictures.

"We're trying to make a portable commode for the troops," one said.

I laughed and said "I'm not going to sit on something like that where everyone can see me taking a crap, especially on the highest point of the mountain!"

They just smiled and went about their business. I told my men about them and we got a good laugh. There was never a dull moment.

All good things must come to an end. Our thirty-day detail was over, and it was time to saddle up and move out. It was late June or early July in 1967. I had the fire team double-check the equipment to make sure we had everything. That meant retrieving the claymore mine we'd put in the barbed wire. We didn't want to leave that behind; it was one of our bread-and-butter defenses.

The last thing we did was burn the trash that had accumulated in a bomb crater. The fire also destroyed the excess items we couldn't carry back down the mountain. The VC was great at using anything and everything against us, so we didn't want to leave them any gifts. As we left the perimeter, a large bang sounded in the fire. We hoped the explosion was just the extra C-ration cans. We never found out for sure, though.

We followed the mountain ridge down to about twenty meters from where I'd taken my recon unit a couple of weeks earlier. We must have gotten soft from being on the mountain for so long with no physical exercise because everyone complained and asked to stop. It took a while before we made it to the bottom and headed toward flat land.

We moved out a mile or two but when I looked back up the mountain, it looked like we hadn't gone far at all. We got word to move another couple of clicks. A B-52 was going to bomb a mountain adjacent to the one we just left.

Up in the blue sky a white streak of smoke cut across the heavens. The B-52 is a Stratofortress jet and usually has a high-explosive ordinance capacity of around 81,000 pounds. Sometimes we heard it after the payload was dropped. The B-52 primarily flew over the DMZ to wipe out the enemy and their artillery.

That day I was going to get a taste of their power.

All of a sudden, this awful wailing and whooshing noise came from above. I'll never forget that sound. Then loud thumping sounds came one after another. On the mountain, dark dirt flew up as much as a hundred feet.

Shrapnel and debris started falling around us. I got down as low as I could to avoid being hit. The shrapnel wasn't small, either. Huge chunks of the mountain rained down. We didn't move. If we had, I'm pretty sure someone would have been hit and seriously injured.

It was over in matter of minutes. Thank God!

Once we got the all-clear, we dusted ourselves off and checked to see if anyone was injured. Then everyone began to chatter in disbelief about how the huge chunks barely missed us. It had been scary.

Our platoon hiked several hours back to the bomb site for a damage report. There might have been a VC headquarters or even an underground hospital in that area, so we needed to confirm the information. As we got closer, everyone commented on the size and depth of the craters. From a distance they looked small but they were huge, maybe fifteen to twenty feet deep.

The ground was still warm, sometimes hot, inside the craters. I assumed the 1,000-pound bombs had caused the large craters and maybe the 500-pound bombs made the smaller ones. The largest was at least half the size of a football field. A whole platoon of Marines could have stood in that crater and still had elbow room.

We counted our blessings that day and realized we were very fortunate no one had been seriously injured by the shrapnel.

Chapter Fourteen
Street without Joy

Back at Camp Evans, we got a few days of recuperation after our long walk down from the mountain. We never knew when or where our next mission would be until we got our evening briefing. Sometimes the platoon sergeant surprised us by bringing beer and soda; the beer was warm but we still thanked him and drank it promptly.

By early July 1967, I'd figured out how the system operated—one company stayed behind to do perimeter watch while two companies went out. In camp, we had bunker watch just about every night but the fire teams alternated this duty. I had bunker duty on July 3 and was told not to pop any flares at midnight when the 4th arrived. They said if we got caught popping flares, we would get office hours the following morning.

That was the term for being punished at the commander's office. In boot camp, the punishments had been more basic. If someone screwed up on the parade deck, the DI marched us behind a Quonset hut and made us do "Up and Arm Shoulders" with a weapon. This meant pumping the rifle out and over your head, sometimes bringing it behind your head. The M-14 weighed 9.1 pounds. It got pretty heavy pretty quickly.

The moves were supposed to strengthen the upper body, shoulders, and arms. I ached all over when we finished. I believed everything we did had a purpose. I wouldn't take anything for granted regarding my training. I was proud of the training I received from my DIs and the Marine Corps.

The night watch went pretty well on July 3; the familiar chanting rose up from the village in the valley below my hole and the sky was clear with extremely bright stars. In the distance Puff was doing its thing with 7.62-mm tracer rounds peppering the ground and flashes of light sparking far to the north.

It wasn't long before someone on my left started popping flares. Since it was green, it might have been the signal that a patrol was coming back through the lines. Then again, it might not have been legitimate. It was nearly midnight when someone on my right popped a white flare. Someone else popped a green one then a red one. Then I heard, "Happy birthday, America!"

The Marines who set off the flares weren't in our unit so I'm not sure if anything happened to them the next morning. But that was the only excitement that whole Fourth of July morning; hardly any fire missions or artillery could be heard. All of a sudden it was very quiet. The villagers probably thought we were crazy with all the flares going off.

I knew exactly why those guys had set off those flares despite the risk of punishment. We were all proud to be there, to be serving our country. That same pride and excitement had been with us probably before we even joined the service. The afternoon I had signed up with the recruiter, I boarded a bus with twelve other Marine enlistees. We caught a flight to San Diego, California to go through boot camp at the MCRD.

That flight on American Airlines was my first ever. It was quite unique—not only was I finally leaving the state where I'd been born and raised; I was doing so on a jet plane. At the San Diego Airport, I was told to line everyone up and move them to the lobby to wait for the DI. Well, it didn't take long before I heard someone yelling, "Stand at attention! Spit that gum out! Put the cigarettes out! Keep your mouth shut!"

The DI was a Caucasian with a medium build and, of course, extra short hair. He wore a Smokey Bear hat with a globe eagle centered at the front. He was very neatly dressed in a brown shirt with sharp creases front and back. His tie sported a Marine Corps clasp and his green trousers also had sharp creases. His black shoes were so shiny they glowed at night.

"Do you hear me?" he bellowed. His voice was very deep and everything he said was spoken with authority.

Actually, he shouted with authority, "Do you hear me?"

All I could think was, "Oh, Lord, I'm not in formation yet."

I wondered what he was going to do to me. He told us to face right, move out in single file, board the buses, and find a seat. "Keep your head and eyes straight to the front and keep them there!" he yelled. "No talking!"

The bus filled up pretty quickly, so some of the recruits turned around and got off. The DI yelled, "Get back on the bus!" at least four times. When a recruit told him it was full, the DI climbed on and yelled for all the extra recruits to move to the end of the aisle. He then said to turn around and sit, starting at the rear.

The first recruit did as he was told and sat down in the middle of the aisle. The next recruit sat on his lap. They went up the row like that and there was plenty of room. I was one of the lucky ones who'd found a seat so I kept quiet.

The DI got off the bus, removed his Smokey, and started rubbing his head. One of the recruits decided to talk but another DI standing just outside heard. The private was pulled off the bus to have his butt chewed. Then he had to do push-ups. After that, I didn't move or blink. Only my eyeballs moved, scanning the terminal and wondering whether I should catch a flight back to Oklahoma.

Maybe I could tell the DI that I wasn't part of this group and I got on the bus by mistake. Even as those thoughts raced through my head, I knew I never would say that. I sure felt sorry for that recruit, though. I don't know about the other guys but I saw nothing the entire ride. It was late enough that it was pitch black outside. Besides, we held our eyes straight to the front as ordered.

Despite this stressful start, the MCRD was an attractive location. It sat on the bay of San Diego across from the airport. The landscape was green with plenty of eucalyptus trees. A huge parade field lay at the center surrounded by tan, Spanish-style stucco offices and classrooms, the commanding general's headquarters, warehouses, an exchange, a receiving area, and rows and rows of steel Quonset huts.

The Quonset huts were used for recruit billeting/barracks. There were also buildings for testing and officer and enlisted clubs. The base had a three-mile running track and an obstacle course which spanned the south end of the base. It also bordered the Naval Training Center. It was a busy place, filled with recruits and others going through boot camp.

The second we pulled into the receiving barrack, the DIs yelled, "Get off the bus! Get off the bus!" at the top of their lungs.

I think we trampled each other getting off. I really don't remember hitting the ground. Suddenly I was standing on the famous yellow footprints painted on the asphalt where so many other recruits have stood. My head and eyes still looked straight ahead. Some recruits were running around looking for their own footprints. A few pushed other men off theirs.

The DIs kept yelling until everyone was on a footprint and standing at attention. We were told to keep our hands and arms at our sides, to keep our feet at a forty-five degree angle, and not to move. That was pretty hard for some folks; they kept leaning back and forth. The DIs ordered those guys to do push-ups.

I don't remember how many push-ups one recruit did. I just knew it was one too many for me.

I kept thinking, "Oh God, oh God, what have I done?"

My hands were getting tired trying to hold them in against the side of my pants while maintaining the slight curl as directed. But after what they did to the other recruits, I decided I could do it.

Another DI came out. He was African American, slender, with the same crisp uniform as the others. He didn't say much and let the first DI do most of the talking — or barking. Eventually he told us to line up through some doors and to keep our mouths shut.

Everything was fine until we saw what was about to happen. In seconds our hair was gone. This was the first step in changing our lives. We all came out of the barber's chair with white heads looking like baby eagles. We all had a good laugh...or I should say a good giggle. We tried to keep quiet so we wouldn't have to do more push-ups.

Once everyone was bald, we filed into a large room filled with chest-high tables. The instructor told us to stand behind a table, remove our clothes, and put them on the table. Then we were hustled into the showers for a quick soaping and rinsing. We dried off, threw the wet towels into a large hamper, and put on our uniforms.

We got the minimum supplies: one yellow sweatshirt with the red USMC emblem, a web belt and buckle, one pair of green wool socks, one pair of white tennis shoes, a green cap, a shaving kit, one towel, one pair of white boxer shorts, and a duffel bag. We put our civilian clothes and any items we didn't want confiscated into wrapping paper to send home. We then received linens and a mattress cover.

We ran outside and got back on the yellow footprints again. The DIs yelled out a command none of us understood so they made us all do push-ups. Once they explained what we were supposed to do, we marched off.

I don't know if it could actually be called marching; we were pretty uncoordinated. When they said left we stepped out with the right. We just could not get our arms and legs working together. The DI had us interlock our arms so we could stay in step. I'm sure we looked like clowns. As a matter of fact, that's what one of the DIs called us...clowns.

At this point we were dog-tired and they were trying to get us to bed. I had no idea what time it was; I just know it seemed very late. As we marched down the streets of MCRD, we heard the jets coming into and out of the San Diego airport. I'm pretty sure we were all thinking the same thing—we wished we were on one of the planes going home.

Finally we arrived at the Quonset huts. The DI counted out the recruits for each hut. I believe there were about eighty in our platoon altogether. He told us to make our bunks, get in them and get some sleep, and no talking.

Some of the recruits, including me, talked in a low whisper. We introduced ourselves and decided who had the top rack or the lower bunk. We had a storage space, a small locker, and another locker to store our equipment and personal items.

"Ladies," the DI said, "the lights are going out."

He hit the switch. I have never heard so many grown men cry in one place in all my life. Some of the guys talked about climbing the fence and going AWOL. Most of the recruits were draftees. Some of the

Hispanic recruits said they'd been in trouble with the law and the judges had told them either to join the military or go to jail.

The recruits were from Texas, Alabama, Arkansas, and Oklahoma. Most came from Tennessee and Kentucky. We had a blast listening to the folks from the Southern states, especially if they had a deep drawl and used Southern slang. They kept us laughing, and we felt like we were at a comedy show.

One of the recruits from Kentucky called one from Tennessee, "Hillbilly." That name fit him like a glove. The laughing and giggling went on for quite some time until a DI pounded on the door. "Any more wisecracks," he hollered, "and you'll be outside doing push-ups!" After that there was total silence.

We all worked hard to earn the right to be part of the military and to serve our country. Even those guys who'd cried their first night in boot camp had become tough, proud Marines. Although nothing beats being at home on the Fourth of July, seeing the various colors of the flares was great. I was proud that the Marines did what they had to do to celebrate Independence Day no matter what we were doing or where we were. It was a night I won't ever forget.

* * *

After a couple of weeks with no mission or operation, it was time for some action. We were getting a little stale sitting around with only bunker watch and classes. Our next assignment seemed simple. Trucks transported us to a location near a village between Quang Tri and a hamlet called Thon My. It looked the same as all the other villages. A bamboo fence ran around the entire area with thatched straw huts inside.

Reports said this village was infested with VC and the villagers supported the guerrilla units. The trucks crossed a bridge next to the village and stopped a few yards north. We jumped off, made a quick head count then marched along the north side of the riverbank heading east. We were to be the blocking force for a unit sweeping the opposite side of the river moving toward us.

We sat behind bamboo and trees in the white sand. We dug in and waited for the VC. The riverbank was low with normal civilian activity all along the water. When a lovely lady washed her legs by the river's edge, one of the Marines let out a whistle. Then we went back to digging a defensive position.

Marines were always looking out for the pretty girls.

Back in boot camp, we'd finally gotten off base when we were sent north for more training. It was our first chance to see what California looked like. We took Old Highway 101 past La Jolla then past Torrey Pines beach. Next came Del Mar and Cardiff by the Sea. The coastline was beautiful.

At that time of morning, a lot of surfers were heading down to the beach with their boards. Someone in the back of the bus said that surfing was a lot of fun, and there were always a lot of great looking women hanging out sunbathing. We all jumped up hoping to catch a glimpse of those pretty girls in their bikinis.

And there we were in the middle of a war doing basically the same thing: jumping at the chance to see a pretty girl. Only in this place, no one ever knew whether the villagers were just going about their business or if we were being set up for an ambush.

After digging for about an hour, the young lady returned and started washing her legs again. This time, the Marine stepped out of the trees and walked toward her to say hello. As soon as he took a couple of steps, she disappeared. A shot rang out from across the river.

A sniper hit the young Marine in the leg. We thought either the girl was shooting or maybe she had drawn us off guard so the sniper could take a shot.

The Marine crawled behind some cover but more sniper fire came at our position. It was sporadic and no one else got hit. Our corpsman provided first aid and requested a medevac chopper. It didn't take long for the birds to arrive. The corpsman rushed the Marine aboard and they were off just like that.

The guy was lucky. The bullet had only hit the meaty part of the leg and had missed the bone. He'd be fine with proper care as long as an infection didn't set in. In the muggy summer heat, wounds could fester quickly and the corpsman had wanted the Marine out of the area fast for just that reason.

No one ventured out after that. Every once in a while we received small arms fire from the village. At one point, our squad leader panicked.

"We're surrounded!" he yelled. "We're pinned down!"

I was lying against a log and turned to have a look at him. Just because we were being sniped at didn't mean we were surrounded.

"It's just small arms fire," I said.

We kept our heads and butts down and dug a little deeper into the sand. We managed to eat our C rations while hunkered down. A lot of gunfire was coming from the other side of the village. It sounded like it was moving toward our positions through the village. It was either the ARVN or one of our forces conducting a sweep.

Suddenly jets were overhead. I thought they were going to provide someone else with close air support but they kept circling us. One of the units across the river must have called them in. We were told to hunker way down.

I got behind an old log and thought, "Not again."

It was bad enough having B-52s drop their ordinance and send shrapnel falling around you but these were jets.

It wasn't long before the F-4 Phantoms came in. The first one flew in along the lay of the river. They knew we were in a blocking position along the river's edge so they dropped napalm instead of their heavy ordinance. I saw the large silver bomb tumble end over end toward the village. Then a yellow-orange glow and the billowing black smoke appeared.

The firefight was getting pretty intense on the other side of the river. Another napalm hit, this time closer to our position. When it burst, the fireball shot out a heat wave that reached across the water. By this time, the whole village was burning. Popping sounds came from the hooches. It sounded like 7.62-mm ammunition, the standard round for the AK-47s, exploding in the fire.

Aside from that, all was quiet. The Phantoms had left. We were very thankful the F-4s hadn't bombed the wrong side of the river; that mistake would have killed us all. The operational sweep was completed later that afternoon with only one wounded in action (WIA) from our company.

Chapter Fifteen
Night Ambush

Soon someone yelled, "Saddle up!" I got my men ready and wondered where we were going this late in the day. We moved back to the road and crossed the bridge. About twenty minutes later, we crossed Highway 1 and moved across open hills toward the mountain following the river to our left.

A raindrop hit my face. I hoped it wouldn't rain. We were supposed to be re-supplied that day but the choppers wouldn't come in during a heavy rain. Re-supply days were great because we usually got hot sauce. If we were lucky, we got some onions, too. Eating those C rations all the time got pretty boring and the sauce and onions helped dress up the meals.

We halted and dug in; we were in an open area where we could see a good distance around the perimeter. If anyone tried to probe our lines, we'd see them. With many men helping, the helicopters were unloaded in no time. We also got our SP box. That was good news for me. Since no one else smoked cigars, I always received plenty.

As usual, all brands of cigarettes were available but Salem and Kool were the favorites. Not many smokers liked the Winstons, Marlboros, Lucky Strikes, Camels, or Pall Malls. I tried smoking the Camels once but got really lightheaded. They were way too strong. I tried Pall Malls but that didn't last long. Some men preferred to get their cigarettes in a box; that kept them from getting crushed and they stayed drier.

All of a sudden the rain started coming down hard. Although I was already wet and cold, I covered up with my poncho. We all sat out in the open like drenched chickens. When the squad leader said we could start a fire, I set about making hot coffee with cocoa and cream.

While some men carried their stoves, others made a lightweight heating plate with small C-ration cans. It was that much less weight to carry and just as functional. I suddenly thought of a great way to get warm and heat up my coffee at the same time. I got out the little portable stove and the matches I stored in plastic. I threw the poncho over myself, the heat tablets, and the coffee...and quickly learned another lesson.

The fumes from the heat tablets went right up my nose. They were so strong I thought I was going to die. My idea for staying dry and making coffee in the rain wasn't good no matter how cold it was. After that, I couldn't wait for morning. I lie in the rain wrapped in my poncho. The only thing I could do was make sure I wasn't in a low area that might flood or where water might run under me while I slept.

Trying to sleep in wet clothes sure was uncomfortable. I woke once to relieve myself. By then, the rain had eased up and my body heat had dried some of my clothes. Daylight finally came but it was still cold and our damp clothes made it worse.

We'd been trained to be comfortable being uncomfortable. At least, the Corps had done its best to teach us to tolerate a lot of things. In addition to the long hours, night exercises and gruelling physical training, they'd made us crawl through mud and dust during live fire exercises. Above all, though, every recruit's nightmare had been the sand pit.

My platoon had been introduced to it on our second day of training. The pit was located by the obstacle course. Someone must have pissed off the DI because we stayed in the sandpits for hours. The DI would holler, "Make snow!" or "Make rain!" and we would throw the sand in the air to make snow or rain.

We also swam in the sand pits...without water. I can still hear those commands being yelled at me today, "On your face, on your back, on your feet, back down again."

There was no sequence to the commands. If someone screwed up or spoke while in formation, we marched over to the sand pits.

Our physical training at PMI was much the same. After evening chow, we ran and ran then did some leg lifts. Finally we crammed into an eight-by-eight foot area filled with sand.

"On your back, on your feet, get back down, on your face."

Then we switched back to leg lifts, counting out loud as we did them. During all this, the DI yelled, "I can't hear you. Do it again, ladies!"

I believe the group of recruits I was with spent more time in the sand pits than anyplace else. Even today, I dread going to the beach with my family. I just don't like feeling sand all over my body.

* * *

In the morning, we were allowed to have a fire again. I made hot coffee and heated up some boned chicken with cheddar cheese and hot sauce for breakfast. The meal kept me energized and warmed me up inside.

We field cleaned our M-16s and were ready to move out. It was still early and we were going to make a quick sweep of the hamlet below. As we got closer to the village, the dogs started barking. They

131

really didn't make much noise but it was enough to alert the villagers that someone was coming.

We saw no movement and assumed people were still sleeping. We lined up and spread out at double arm's length to wait. A lot of punji stakes, sharpened pieces of bamboo, were set up all over the area. I wondered if they completely surrounded the village. Some of the stakes were in fighting holes so if anyone fell or jumped in, they'd be out of commission for a while.

We thought there might be more booby traps so we became even more alert for signs of trip-wires. When we received the word, we slowly and quietly moved through the village. We'd been informed that tunnels might be hidden in the hamlet but after a quick search of all the hooches, we found nothing.

Around mid-morning we headed to the mountains. We marched in a staggered column keeping about fifteen feet between each man, and it took all day to reach the base of the mountain. From there, we hiked single-file. That allowed each Marine to follow the trail of the person in front.

During the march, it began to get dark. The tall trees blocked out the sun and sometime later we stopped for the night. The platoon guide placed us in our defensive positions. We were ready to start digging when I was summoned by the platoon sergeant. The skipper wanted a squad sent out on an ambush site and it was my turn.

Before it got too dark, I pulled my men together and briefed them. I also told them to tie down any loose objects so they wouldn't rattle. One of my Marines, an African-American, volunteered to walk point. At first I hesitated. He was very dark-skinned and I was afraid I wouldn't be able to see him. I told him so but he wanted to do it so bad.

He was a good Marine and I wanted to give him the chance to walk point even though it worried me. At Camp Pendleton, California, the staging battalion had given me a month of combat training. One class was Escape and Evasion, where we pretended we were captured.

The first thing was to set up a command structure in our group. We had no food except what they gave us to cook for ourselves, such as carrots, onions, and maybe some rice. What they gave us had to feed a hundred men. Later in the night, some of the instructors took on the role of aggressors. We had to escape and evade in groups as we moved along the dark confines of Camp Pendleton, hiding behind brush and sneaking back to our bivouac area miles away.

I had been trained to know what to do if I was ever captured but I'd hoped that would never happen. Every time we went on patrol, we risked being caught in a firefight or being captured. I didn't want to lose this Marine or any of my men during the night. We had to do our duty and mine was getting those men back safe.

Finally I said, "Okay, but make sure you stay kind of close."

He just laughed. It was very dark by this time and the thick jungle made visibility worse. Heavy vegetation grew to our right and tall trees flanked our left. The trees dangled branches over our heads, so that cut out even what little light we might otherwise have had from the stars.

Our point man moved slowly but I couldn't see him. It was so dark we couldn't even see our own hands. We had to take a few steps, stop, and listen over and over. When illumination flares went off in the lowland some distance away, just enough light filtered through the canopy to allow us to move.

To keep track of each other, I had the men touch each other's backs. When the illumination flares stopped, I whispered for the point man to stop. As we sat on the trail, I said, "Slow down just a hair. I can't see you without the light from the flares."

We were about thirty minutes out from the camp when I heard movement on our left. We all hunkered down to listen for whom or

133

what was making the noise. The noise had also stopped so eventually we started moving again.

The minute we got up, we heard it again. I halted the team but the point man didn't hear me. I whispered his name but he still didn't respond. I told the squad to stay put while I went to find him. I kept hissing for him until he finally stopped.

"I heard that noise," he said, "but it sounded like it was behind me. I thought the rest of the squad was making that noise."

When he realized it wasn't us, he got scared. Once we moved back with the squad, I told the radio man to let the CP know there was movement to our left flank. Then we heard movement on our right flank. It sounded like someone walking through the jungle and stopping every now and then.

"Let me throw a grenade," one whispered.

"No," I said. "I don't want it hitting a tree and bouncing back on us."

At that thought, he quieted down. Just as I was getting ready to say something, we heard this big firefight on the other side of the company. I heard grenades or M-79s going off, and there was a lot of chatter on the radio.

The shots were from another ambush patrol. The CP ordered us to come back. We turned around and made our way back up the mountain to the perimeter. We didn't hear the noise after the firefight. Whoever or whatever it was must have run off or kept quiet while we moved out.

After I briefed the platoon sergeant, I told the men they could sleep there or go back to their holes. We all decided to stay put. The CO ordered the squad leader to sweep for a body count as soon as daylight came. We all thought we'd get good news. We'd heard there might have been a VC base camp in the area, and I thought for sure we'd caught them off guard for a change.

When daylight broke through the tall trees, the ground was wet with dew and the air was slightly foggy. It wasn't long before I heard a lot of laughing at the CP. The platoon guide said there was a body count all right...for a bunch of rock apes. The batutut, "forest people believed to have walked the remote lands of Vietnam," didn't stand a chance in the firefight.

That was our laugh for the day. The entire patrol got a lot of teasing for a job well done. We had to have a sense of humor to stay sane under the conditions. Everyone took it in stride. We always reminded ourselves we were lucky not to be casualties.

Still, out there in the dark, our patrol was like a bunch of kids scared by the regular sounds of the night.

In grade school, I played on a great basketball team with two of my first cousins. Since we played against each other after school, we knew each other's moves and shot selections.

As our team got stronger, we won quite a few championship trophies from grade school through high school. For out-of-town games, we walked to the school and caught a bus. When we returned home late at night, we walked home in the darkness. Sometimes we caught a ride. If not, we walked in the pitch black.

During those walks we always seemed to hear things we normally didn't hear. We tried to spook each other by pretending to be scared of some unknown thing stalking around in the dark. One night we overdid it.

"Did you hear that?" someone asked. "What was that noise? It sounds like someone's walking behind us."

We turned to look. Even though nothing was there, we were so scared we took off at a full sprint. That thing was not going to catch us!

We probably heard pebbles being kicked up by our shoes. At least, I hoped so. After running a ways, we finally stopped to catch our breath. The family dogs started barking so we knew we were safe. So much for being macho!

Once the laughter and ribbing from the other Marines died down, we were given the nod to start a fire. I looked for something sensible to make for breakfast. I still had a lot of different jellies from our stay on Recon Mountain, and they were good on toasted bread with peanut butter. Since I really liked strong, rich-tasting coffee, I always doubled the packets to give it more flavor...just like back home.

It was a nice morning even though there was a little fog. As the sunlight pierced the tall jungle trees, the mist lifted. In the far distance lay the mountains and valleys. Somewhere over there that ghost rooster was crowing his lungs out. Everyone was in a good mood from all the joking.

After our meal, we waited to move out but it seemed like no one was in a hurry. I wondered which platoon, squad, and fire team was going to walk point today. Finally, we got the word to saddle up. Our lead was Second Platoon; my friends who'd joined the company with me were in that platoon. I hadn't seen them in quite a while and wondered how they were doing.

We moved out on the winding trails down the mountain. All of a sudden, the company stopped. Second Platoon had found some empty hooches nestled against the side of the mountain. We spread out and moved toward the campsite. The place looked fairly new. There was a long building with mats on the deck, probably where the VC slept. Other buildings were scattered throughout the area.

In one hut stood a storage bin filled with rice. We were told to destroy the rice any way we could. It turns out that rice is impossible to burn. We had to do whatever we could to destroy the VC food supply.

Some men urinated on the rice as we dumped it out and scattered it around. Engineers would destroy the buildings using C-4 explosives as we left.

Before we could move out, the radio said that the lead platoon had spotted a couple of VC coming up the trail. They sent a squad to set up a hasty ambush. Since my platoon was farther up the mountain, we sat down to wait.

Soon we heard gunfire. It sounded like all hell had broken loose, like the whole company was involved. The M-60 machine gun was singing Dixie, grenades were exploding or someone was using an M-79 grenade launcher, and M-16s cracked and popped. Everything echoed through the jungle.

It was over in minutes. I thought for sure we'd have a good body count or at least a few prisoners. But evidently someone in the ambush had an itchy trigger finger. His burst of M-16 rounds missed the target. When everyone heard that M-16, they all opened fire.

Those two VC had turned around in mid-step and high-tailed it back down the trail. Everyone laughed. The incident wasn't really funny but the way it was relayed over the radio made us laugh. I could just see those VC running like scared rabbits, jumping over rocks and branches with their arms flopping in the wind.

I bet the young Marine who'd fired too early wouldn't get R&R any time soon. We figured it might have been cooks or some other support personnel headed up to the base camp. We got the call to move out and continued down the trail. It was now around the first or second week of August 1967. It took all day but finally we descended to flat terrain. The CH-53s lifted us back to Camp Evans. After mail call, I went back into my routine—clean my 782 gear and weapon, take a shower, and wait for the next mission.

Chapter Sixteen
Ambush on the Road

For the next few days, we took it kind of easy. Most of the time, we attended classes on map reading, medevac procedures, and the like. Reviewing all those lessons and thinking back on the experiences in the bush, it was amazing to realize how far we'd come since our raw recruit days.

My first morning in boot camp, I'd gone to the mess hall. A DI stood by the tray station telling each recruit what to eat. The obese privates had toast, fruit and skim milk. The skinny recruits were told to get a lot of food and to eat everything they took. I was in between so whatever I put on my tray was okay.

We got our food, marched to the tables, slid sideways along the benches, and set our trays on the table. When everyone was present, the DI yelled, "Ready! Seat!

There was this loud thundering as we tried to sit in unison. The DI wasn't happy. He yelled, "Get up, ladies! All together now, ladies. Ready! Seat!"

We did this for perhaps five minutes. When we were finally allowed to eat, we had about two minutes to finish. We stuffed food into our mouths like steam shovels. Some of the privates were still eating when the DI yelled, "Get out! Get out!"

My mouth was full of eggs as I stood up with everyone else. We left our trays at the dishwashing station and ran outside to stand in something like a formation. This was our first morning together so the rows were pretty ragged. A DI put us in the correct formation.

Sometimes during all the weeks of training, my thoughts went back to Oklahoma. I wondered what I would have been doing if I'd stayed home. Would I have been out of a job and looking for a new one without any money in my pocket? Could I have survived on minimum wages and continued to do the same old thing over and over? Just how far would I have been able to go in life if I hadn't joined the Corps?

I also wondered if I'd made the right decision. I guess I'd been searching for something but I didn't know what. When I thought about it, I felt I had made the right choice. The first month of the "God-forsaken boot camp training" wasn't as bad as I'd expected so maybe I was up to the challenge.

Training was long and hard but I learned a lot that would allow me to survive in combat. After that was done, I received a certificate to prove I was a full-fledged Marine Corps infantryman. My orders were to report to Basic Infantry Training at Camp San Mateo. I couldn't believe it.

I said, "More infantry training? What else is there to learn?"

The Marine Corps gave me some good training and I enjoyed every bit of it. What we put into it was what we got back. A sign in camp said, "The more you sweat, the less you bleed." I believed firmly in that saying. So even during the slow times in Vietnam, we paid attention to the refresher courses and learned from our mistakes.

* * *

One afternoon, the platoon sergeant mentioned we might be heading north for a change. The men asked all sorts of questions but he said he didn't know anything more and to just be patient. Later that

139

evening, he gave us an update. Our platoon was going to run patrols north of Camp Evans in an area a little south of Quang Tri City.

The next morning, we would leave Camp Evans for good and work our way toward Dong Ha. Our company office would also relocate there soon. Dong Ha was one of the base camps and was known as Leatherneck Square. It had gotten that name due to the number of Marines massed in that area and around Con Thien, Gio Linh and Cam Lo.

Camp Carroll was outside Cam Lo and Rockpile was northwest of Cam Lo. Khe Sahn was farther out, situated toward the mountain range near the Laotian border. I had been in Vietnam for four months by then. I still had a long way to go before my days were over...but who was counting?

* * *

Early the next day, trucks roared up the dirt road toward Camp Evans bringing a cloud of red dust into camp. The dust was so heavy, it settled on everything. I took my usual spot in the rear of the truck. By looking straight ahead, I could see everyone on the truck and along both sides of the road.

The drive took more than two hours. It would have been faster but we had to slow down for all the Vietnamese nationals using Highway 1. There were small vans and cars loaded with people everywhere. Their arms hung out the windows to catch any breeze. Bikes dotted the edge of the road and occasionally a water buffalo or horse would be pulling a cart.

When I was about six, we had two white horses. The mare had a colt which my brother trained and rode. I guess he needed some quick money because he ended up selling the colt for a few bucks. I still remember the horses' names, Ol' Maude and Ol' Frank. They were good animals. One time I fell asleep while riding and the horse took me home. The last time I had seen them was when they were hitched to a wagon for a wood-hauling trip. My Dad would take the team into the back woods to gather seasoned firewood for heating and cooking. When I returned from boarding school, they told me both horses had died.

Now I was headed for a new home farther north in Vietnam. We passed several small hamlets, and as usual, vendors sat all along the highway. Our trucks never stopped. It was getting very hot with the sun beating down so I adjusted the towel around my neck. The terrain was flat with scattered shrubbery and small mounds of white sand dunes.

The trucks stopped in a place called Hai Lang in the Quang Tri providence. Hai Lang was a small town that sat beside the highway. Most of the buildings looked like they were made of white stucco. I didn't look around much because it was so hot that I kept my face shaded under a towel.

The building we pulled in front of looked like a city hall or some other official digs. It was white and had several steps leading up to the porch. The whole area was sandy, and we sat around waiting. Looking north up Highway 1, there was nothing but white sand on both sides of the highway, kind of like a giant sand pit transplanted from boot camp.

Children gathered around us saying, "Marines number one," and, "G.I.s number one." We gave the kids C-ration candies and other food most Marines didn't eat like the date pudding and fruit cakes.

By noon the sun was really beating down. It was too hot to even guess how hot it was. I soaked my towel with water from my canteen and draped it over my helmet with both hands to create some shade.

Blistering heat radiated up off the white sand. No matter what I did, there was just no relief.

Usually when we arrived in a village, people came out in droves to sell us stuff. Here only a handful of people showed up. Even the number of children was a lot less than normal. The Vietnamese children thought I was an interpreter so they didn't bother me much. Although I didn't mind them, sometimes it was nice to be left alone. There were times it paid to be a Native American.

I was beginning to wonder why it was taking so long for the platoon to move out. It must have been around 1400 hours when the platoon sergeant said we'd move up Highway 1 in a staggered column on both sides of the road. Our destination was about five kilometers from Hai Lang City.

With the hot sun beating down and the heat washing up in waves from the ground, we headed out. The sand seemed to go on for miles. When we reached our destination, the platoon guide placed everyone in a 360 defensive position. Highway 1 was the front of the perimeter. We had only two squads, maybe thirty to forty men total.

My team was assigned to the rear of the perimeter. It was almost impossible to dig a deep fighting hole because the sand kept falling back in the hole, but I told the men to dig deep enough to fire lying down. Considering that we only had a single platoon, the perimeter was stretched pretty thin. To top it off, one squad had to go out to set up an ambush.

Up near the highway behind some sand dunes, the M-60 machine gun was set up; there was also a team of rockets with ammo humpers there. Another machine-gun team was going out with the ambush patrol. Taking that squad, about fourteen Marines, from our 360-defensive perimeter left us with just a handful of men.

The VC was thought to travel through the area transporting supplies. Our goal was to ambush and destroy or disrupt them. We had all the areas covered and were ready. The sun was starting to go down and it was getting a little cooler but not much. I told the men to eat now because the night might be a long one. They were concerned about our defensive position and threw out all kinds of what-ifs.

I assured them we had enough firepower to repel any force, especially with our claymore mine. Plus we could see each other. The bad part was that our one-man fighting holes were only eight to ten feet apart.

If anything moved in front of us, we knew it wasn't friendly. We all sat waiting. That's all we could do–sit in the heat and wait. We were very anxious for the sun to go down.

Before dark, the patrol went a couple kilometers along Highway 1 looking for an ambush site. From radio reports a man in a rice paddy had been sighted. Some of the Vietnamese men were farmers during the day and VC guerilla fighters at night. When the Marines tried to ask him a few questions, he ran toward the mountains. Despite getting a warning shot, the guy kept running and got away.

The patrol eventually located an ambush site under a bridge that had a lot of foot traffic during the day. The platoon sergeant then held a squad leaders' meeting.

"We're spread thin so we really need to stay alert and watch each other's backs," he said. "We're in a heavily traveled VC area for supply transport and for travel toward the seacoast...probably for a little R&R."

We laughed, grateful for a little joke to relieve the tension.

Our job was to secure the area, and to run patrols and ambushes from this location. It looked like my team's position at the rear of the perimeter was a good one. I headed back to give the men the password. Lying in the white sand, which was still warm, we went on high alert.

Night fell. The ambush patrol headed out. The Marines guarding the perimeter were ready. The moonlight and stars were bright that night. The white sand reflected some light even in the darkness, and we watched the patrol move up Highway 1.

It was close to the end of August by then, or maybe as late as the first week of September. Believe it or not, I'd lost count of the days and weeks and how much time I had left in my tour. As the moon disappeared, I thought about where I'd be on a night like this in Oklahoma and what I'd be doing. More than likely I'd be in a soft bed with the air conditioner on.

It was a little past midnight when I heard someone behind our position talking. I could see across the perimeter, and a figure stood up from behind a sand dune. My first thought was that it was a Marine making a head call. When the shadow jumped toward the front of the perimeter, a shot rang out. The Marine went down.

The M-60 machine gun and small arms immediately opened fire. Illumination flares popped off around the area. I looked to the front, rear, and both flanks. The front edge fired at a column of VC scattering in every direction. They didn't have a clue where we were, and the troops continued to fire as the intruders dispersed.

At the time, no one in the platoon knew just how large a unit we encountered. All I remember was the sound of a lot of footsteps behind me. People ran everywhere trying to get away. I thought maybe the VC had entered our perimeter but I didn't see anyone inside our line. I told my men to look all around and stay alert.

Illumination flares kept the area well-lit most of the evening. If the enemy had come inside the perimeter, we would have seen them. Fat chance we'd ever let the VC inside. Once we repelled them, Puff the

Magic Dragon flew in. Everyone was pretty shook up but Puff dropped illumination flares all around us.

The plane flew about a half kilometer west where the pilot spotted a large concentration of enemy troops scattering on foot. The AC-47 let loose with several bursts from its mini-guns. The stream of tracer rounds was continuous. With 6,000 rounds per minute flying down, there were bound to be some serious casualties. We could hear the coils of the guns whirling away as flares dropped at the same time.

After being in the air for quite some time, the pilot had to refuel. He said he'd be back as soon as possible. I was hoping another AC-47 would relieve him but it doesn't work that way. I prayed he'd return quickly.

It seemed like hours but finally we heard the roar of an aircraft engine. An illumination flare lit up the area and there Puff was, ready to spit fire. I sighed in relief because I was running low on illumination flares. I assumed others were, too. If the VC could figure out where we were, we would have been overrun and wiped out. Others were thinking the same thing.

We were all pretty much in shock after that firefight. A corpsman called for a medevac for one downed Marine. Puff was still dropping illumination flares when a CH-34 came in with its lights on. That was the first time I'd seen a helicopter with its lights on since I'd arrived in Vietnam. As the medevac left, we all prayed that Marine would make it to the hospital ship anchored off the coast.

We stayed awake all night. As the hours passed, I hoped Puff wouldn't leave. The aircraft and all the illumination flares were like a security blanket. My men were getting sleepy but we stayed alert until near dawn. By that time, Puff had informed us there were no more activities nearby. I called the fire team in and we took turns napping.

We didn't know if the contact that night had been with the NVA or a mix of VC and NVA. We only knew there had been a large concentration of enemy forces. Whoever they were, we surprised them. I sure would have liked to personally thank that pilot and buy him and his crew members a drink. They were our saviors that night.

Before returning to our location, the ambush squad made a sweep to review the damage. I'd heard the VC used some type of meat hook to drag their dead and wounded away. They took their dead to keep U.S. intel from getting an accurate body count. It was also meant to keep our troops from building morale by not being able to see how much damage we'd done.

That night, we got a little satisfaction. The patrol squad said it was a huge mess out there. It looked like a lot of bodies had been dragged through the sand. The amount of blood on the white sand proved that many VC had been wounded or killed. Some bodies had been left behind. It appeared they had tried to drag them off but couldn't because their arms were ripped apart.

* * *

After an early chow of C rations, we sat around. Before the sun came out and it got too hot, I drank some coffee to keep myself awake. Traffic was beginning to flow along the highway as more Vietnamese from the city went by. Security was still a big concern so someone always stood watch while others slept. We argued over who would stand watch first, just like little kids, but kids who'd been through ferocious firefights.

The rest of the company convoy showed up an hour later. They were full of questions about the night's events. A couple of empty trucks arrived to pick us up. I took my usual position at the rear and we rolled north. Our next mission was to relieve another battalion of Marines in that area.

Right then, though, we were headed for a base camp with an artillery unit. I believe it was a detachment of Marines from the Twelfth Artillery Unit; they were at a fire support base called C-2 located just north of Dong Ha and outside of Cam Lo. We were getting pretty close to the DMZ, the 17th parallel where the North was divided from the South.

Chapter Seventeen
The DMZ

By now it was around the twelfth of September. I'd been reading the Stars and Stripes, the military's newspaper, since I arrived in country. It seemed to be the only news source we had. I read that Con Thien was getting hit almost daily with 152-mm artillery and sometimes with 140-mm rockets and mortars. The fire came from across the DMZ.

We were on our way to Dong Ha, which lay north on Highway 1. The ride was smooth. We passed through Quang Tri City and kept going. Someone yelled out, "There's Dong Ha!" but the trucks flew past. By the amount of red dirt flying everywhere, I knew CH-46s and CH-53s were either landing or taking off from the area. Lots of tents were lined up there, too.

We made a left and headed west on Highway 9. Along that stretch of road, we must have hit every pothole. Heading north again, we passed Cam Lo and crossed a bridge that I assumed spanned the Cam Lo River. We ran out of pavement and kept traveling, leaving a heavy trail of red dust behind.

We were on the downward slope of the C-2, away from the DMZ, when we pulled inside the perimeter. The minute the truck stopped, the driver told us to get off as quickly as possible. He didn't want to be a target for the NVA spotters.

We jumped off and moved downhill. Someone shouted for us to spread out when I heard "Boom, Ba-boom, Boom."

Someone yelled, "Incoming!"

I ran to the nearest trench as the rest of the men scattered for other shelters. My trench was at least six feet deep. Two other Marines flew in behind me, both staff non-commissioned officers (SNCOs). One was a gunnery sergeant and the other a staff sergeant.

They didn't realize how deep the trench was and almost broke their necks tumbling in. Next thing I knew they were laughing at themselves; it was kind of hilarious.

One said, "I saw this on TV once in a combat film—jumping into a fox hole. Now I can't believe it's happening to me."

I was thinking that same thing, "I can't believe it's happening to me. It all seems like a dream."

We just sat at the bottom of the trench laughing.

Then someone yelled, "All clear!"

When I looked around, I didn't see much. We were on the south end of C-2. The platoon sergeant lined everyone up and we moved through the trench along the right side of the perimeter toward the front. The front of C-2 actually faced Con Thien. As we marched, the platoon sergeant dropped squads off at their positions.

My fire team faced north-northeast. Again, here came the "boom, ba-boom." On hearing the first explosion, I turned and saw three greenish rounds heading toward us. They landed near the artillery several yards from our position. Just as the round went off, our battery sent a round in return.

The artillery exchanged fire for a while. It ended with the U.S. firing most of the rounds across the DMZ. Instead of getting a twenty-one gun salute, the Second Battalion, Fourth Marines received a seven-gun salute.

I thought, "What a way to welcome Marines to their new home!"

I counted my blessings yet again because there was never any way to know where the first round would land. It could have easily landed in the trench with me.

After that, the evening was quiet without any incoming. Even then, we kept our heads low and continued to peek out over the firing pits. Some aiming stakes had been placed in the hole; these were used to line up our direction of fire. I hadn't seen those since basic training.

A huge sandbagged bunker stood between every other hole. I was lucky because there was a bunker to my left not far from the north gate. The perimeter was triple-strung with tangle-foot barbed wire plus razor-blade concertina. For a full forty yards beyond that, the area was dense with landmines.

From the inside edge of the barbed wire to the bunkers lay twenty yards of clear space, which gave us good visibility. Any enemy who tried to crawl through our lines would be spotted right away. I seriously doubted anyone would ever try, though.

Whenever anyone moved around inside the compound, we used the trench line. The head was at the south end and my team was on the north. I tried not to go during the day and waited until dark unless it was a real emergency. Some Marines got brave after a while and started walking across the compound...but at a very hurried pace. Not me. I played it safe and used the trenches. My men did the same.

We were four miles south of Con Thien. A dirt road led up there, and a wide path had been cleared on both sides of the road to prevent anyone from setting up an ambush. Several kilometers to the right of Con Thien was Gio Linh where a 175-mm artillery battery provided fire support. I didn't know if we'd be able to use those big guns for close fire support. A single round weighed nearly 150 pounds and was strong enough to wipe out a company.

For a couple of days we pulled sentry duty, guard watch, from our sandbag bunkers. Sometime around September 14, we got our orders. It was time for us to leave the compound.

* * *

I don't remember which company led that morning but we spread out as we marched out of C-2. Earlier that morning, the engineers had performed a mine sweep of the road with an M-48 tank. Being new to that area, I assumed everything was fine for our travel. Then I was told that the NVA was skilled at laying mines during the night without anyone noticing.

We were spread out at least twenty paces as we moved down the road. We didn't want to bunch up and give any NVA gunners a large target. We passed another unit coming in, possibly the Marines we were relieving. One stood out like a sore thumb. I recognized him from our duty as security guards in Bremerton, Washington.

I yelled a greeting and he recognized me. He asked me what unit I was with, and I told him the 2/4. He was with 3/3. He told me to keep my head down as we continued our separate ways. What a small world to see someone from the states in the DMZ.

We finally headed into the thick vegetation to the left side of the road.

I heard "Boom, Ba-boom, Boom" and saw a barrage of 152-mm artillery rounds headed toward us.

I faintly heard our artillery respond. We didn't know whether to hit the ground or continue moving and get out of sight. Someone yelled for us to move out. If we didn't, the enemy would pick us off like sitting ducks.

Our artillery must have been right on target because the NVA fire stopped suddenly. Unfortunately, we'd already taken some losses. The initial rounds had hit the lead company. It took us a while but we finally made it through to where the dead and wounded Marines were sprawled everywhere.

I'd never seen anything like it. That was my first time seeing so many dead and wounded Marines. These were my brothers. Some had their intestines protruding out of the bodies, some were missing limbs. The few who'd survived lie there moaning.

A couple of corpsmen were left behind to give aid and identify the dead. A small number of other Marines also stayed back to provide security. It was heartbreaking to see them lying there. I tried not to look but the thick shrubs on both sides of the trail forced us to step over the bodies of our brothers.

We moved out before the NVA opened fire again. I wanted badly to stop and help those men but knew I could not. I'm certain other Marines were thinking the same thing. Someone yelled to keep moving, to get out of the killing zone.

We patrolled the supply road leading up to Con Thien. It was a wide and dangerous area, a good place to be sniped at, and I was surprised we didn't get hit as we crossed. We made it into the thick vegetation where the lead company found a trail. Weaving between and around shrubs, we patrolled southeast of Con Thien heading in a northeasterly direction.

In the early afternoon, we passed banana groves where some of the trees were twenty feet tall. Without warning, the "plump, plump, plump" of incoming rounds sounded. I didn't know where it was coming from but we had to take cover immediately. The platoon scattered for the nearest holes; then the deadly NVA mortars fell all around us.

As the shells peppered the area, I ran back to a hole I'd seen earlier and jumped in. I ended up a few yards away from the rest of the platoon. Sitting there by myself I could only hope I didn't get overrun or captured.

The mortar barrage was still coming in pretty hard. I sat there peeking over the rim in all directions to avoid any unwanted surprises. I took off the rifle's safety in case I had to shoot my way out.

At the same time, we heard a barrage of mortar and rockets hitting Con Thien. We'd been told that the Third Battalion, Ninth Marines were inside Con Thien with the Second Battalion, Ninth Marines sitting southeast of the perimeter.

When the barrage stopped, I raced back to the platoon. Someone yelled, "Corpsman up!"

I hadn't realized I'd been hit by shrapnel. It was a miracle that it was only a gash. The platoon sergeant said to see if anyone else was hurt. We only suffered a few flesh wounds and some other minor dings. The corpsman patched everyone up and we moved out quickly. We'd all been lucky; it could have been worse.

With the few hours of daylight left, Golf Company conducted a patrol several hundred yards southeast of Con Thien. It was a large sweep. That was September 19, 1967. We had to be on our toes in case we got another barrage of incoming mortar or artillery rounds. We all hoped the rounds didn't have our names on them.

After we found an area that looked defensible, the battalion set up in a night defensive position. We moved the companies into an area of trees that looked like pecan groves. By this time, the sky had turned overcast and was getting dark. My team sat on the western side of the perimeter. I thought the trees would help shield us from mortar attacks yet there was enough open terrain to see anyone crawling in on our perimeter.

The tall trees and the area reminded me of home. Once, my cousin and I picked pecans on someone else's property. My cousin said he'd gotten permission but he actually didn't. We got out of there pretty quick before the owner showed up with a shotgun. We made just enough money from selling those pecans to buy gas, a cheeseburger and a Coke.

There would be no hot burgers for me that night. As we dug in, the rains came; it was pouring. I threw on my poncho and tried to find something I could eat quickly. I sure would have liked some beans and franks but I didn't have any. I found something else and made do.

I thought the rain would let up after about an hour but I was dead wrong. Everyone had talked about the monsoon and now I was getting my first taste of the heavy rains.

The corpsman said, "Keep your feet as dry as possible and change your socks often."

Since I was headed out for an ambush patrol that night, well, so much for keeping my feet dry.

Meanwhile, the squad tried to stay dry under their ponchos. We kept our M-16s under the ponchos, too. The rain made it chilly and night was falling. First Squad, my squad, was doing the ambush patrol with reinforcements from Second Squad. The weapons section had assigned us an M-60 machine-gun detachment. We stood in the pouring rain counting heads to ensure we returned with the same number.

Our ambush patrol moved out in a northwest direction and found a good area between Con Thien and the battalion. Everyone was griping about the weather. We didn't mind the assignment but the rain really bugged us. We were getting soaked under our ponchos.

When the squad leader said to sit in, someone asked, "Are we going to lie on the ground in all this water?"

I almost laughed out loud because I knew that was our only choice. We got down in the mud and about four inches of water.

The M-60 machine gun covered the area north of our position. Then we waited, really for two things—one, for the rain to stop and two, for the NVA to show.

We were still hunkered down when the rain pounded even harder. Our clothes, socks, and boots were soaked. The pool of water grew to at least twelve inches deep. It felt like we were lying in a creek bed.

Then the ants hit. They must have been trying to get out of the rising water. They crawled all over us, biting the heck out of some of us. It was a terrible night. We thought the NVA wouldn't be out on a night like that; if they were, they were crazy.

Finally, the radio man received a call and we were able to get up very carefully and head back to our company area. By then we were freezing. When we approached the perimeter and gave the password, we moved inside and conducted a head count. Everyone was present.

Since we didn't have to perform radio watch, we found a spot to settle in. Sleep was difficult, however, with the continuous rain and our wet clothes. I wrapped up inside my poncho and tried to sleep sitting up or leaning against my pack.

We were fortunate not to have had contact with the NVA during our ambush patrol. The troops were facing a larger force of NVA regulars in the northern sector of Vietnam compared to the southern region. We were operating just south of the DMZ in an area called the Trace, a wide strip running between Con Thien and Gio Linh.

Our job was to deny the NVA entry into the South and the populated areas. We had to stop the NVA from terrorizing the population where we were trying to win people over to our side. But up here, a battalion-sized force often faced off a regiment or division of NVA regulars.

The main division we were concerned with was the 324B. That area had a couple of regiments around where we were patrolling. The terrain was flat with a lot of shrubbery and small trees, and it constantly amazed me how the enemy could hide such a large unit there. The NVA was very good at camouflage and also very elusive.

We stayed just south of the Trace for a couple of days conducting patrols. Almost every day, we heard the continuous bombardment of Con Thien. Rockets, artillery, and mortar fire peppered that hill. The Marines suffered heavy casualties that year during the heavy fighting. I wondered if we were going to be next. It was too close for comfort.

For now, things were all right. No one had complained about the situation in the DMZ, just the rain. Our morale was good and even though we were shelled every now and then, we took it in stride. We always thanked God when we made it through another day.

Chapter Eighteen
The Battle of September 21, 1967

There could be no honor in a sure success,
but much might be wrested from a sure defeat.
T.E. Lawrence, English Marine and author (1888-1935)

It was late September 1967, just an ordinary morning, and I began my regular daily routine. There was no incoming mortar or rocket fire pounding our position for a change, and the chilled air from the night still lingered. I was still damp from sleeping under my poncho following night patrol. With the cool morning breeze, it could be quite cold. I was a little tired and hungry, but woke to what was supposed to be another ordinary day.

It was partly cloudy but cleared up around 0700 hours, earlier than it normally did. I got the other men on my team up. I could hear mumbling throughout the camp so everyone was beginning to stir. My C-ration selection was limited so I used what was available to make breakfast and began drinking my coffee.

After about half an hour, everyone had finished chow and started cleaning their M-16s, mandatory after each rainfall. It was peaceful, and looking at the wide-open area got me to wondering how it had been cleared. Had the Marine engineers or Navy Seabees been involved in bulldozing the mile-wide clearing from the mountains to the coast along the DMZ? Whoever was responsible did an incredible job of clearing the shrubs and trees. It gave us such a great advantage because we could see the enemy if they came out in the clear. Still, beyond that area were more tree lines and shrubbery. Although we couldn't see them beyond that point, we knew many dangers lay ahead and we could detect the enemy's movement at the outpost.

The squad leaders were summoned by the platoon sergeant for a morning briefing. The information passed on was that a regiment of NVA was in the southern portion of the DMZ. Any patrols that went out had to be reinforced with additional troops. The battalion's mission that morning was to search and destroy.

Fox Company would conduct a patrol to the east of our battalion perimeter. Echo Company would work to the left of Fox with both companies patrolling east toward Highway 561 outside of Phu Oc. Golf Company would patrol the southeast and sweep northeast to join up with Fox and Echo companies. Hotel Company would be held in reserve and provide security for the CP.

Since this was only a day patrol, we left our packs behind. Our canteens were full of water and we waited with our flak jackets on for the call. As the daylight broke through the fog, the word came to head out. As I put on my helmet, I thought it might be a good day after all, since the fog was lifting earlier than usual.

First Platoon was in the lead heading down a cart path. It was a typical morning patrol, and we kept our distance between each person and staggered the columns. The trail was sandy with patches of grass, and the sun peeked out from behind the clouds. A hint of blue skies began to show. I was already getting a little warm.

As I moved down the path, I noticed a lot of banana trees and rows of hedges in the area. It was probably around 0830 hours when the first shots rang out; they sounded liked AK-47s. The shots grew louder as we moved toward the sound. Then grenades, probably from an M-79 grenade launcher, exploded. The sound echoed through the trees.

All of sudden, a tremendous firefight was taking place. Grenades exploded left and right, and machine guns fired without letting up. It was going to be a long firefight.

The company halted on the cart path. We stood there listening to the explosives and trying to listen to the radio for commands. There was a lot of chatter on the radio, all non-stop and getting louder.

The NVA were entrenched in the hedge rows and had set up a huge ambush. Fox Company walked right into the ambush and was under intense hostile fire. They had been hit pretty hard. Automatic weapons and small arms fire were coming in from all directions. The Marines were pinned down and needed assistance immediately.

Echo Company went in as reinforcement. By then Fox Company was taking on tremendous casualties from incoming mortar rounds. Golf Company was ordered in to provide assistance to both companies. We knew we needed to save our Marines.

The firefight seemed a few feet away, but it was more like a quarter mile off in the distance. We marched forward, anticipating being hit so we picked up our pace. As we jogged down the cart path, our M-16s jingled whenever our loose slings hit our cartridge belts and magazine pouches.

As we neared the area, the company halted. I knelt down, breathing pretty hard after the short sprint. The explosives were getting louder but I couldn't tell whether they were from M-79 grenade launchers or men throwing grenades. For that matter, it could have been mortar rounds falling on our Marines.

I have a faint recollection of receiving orders to fix bayonets, which was odd as it was the first time since I arrived in Vietnam that we were putting our bayonets on our rifles. The fighting was in close quarters and getting pretty intense.

The command came to face left and to move out slowly. I told my men to glance out of the corner of their eyes, stay on line, and maintain a good distance from each other as we moved toward the fighting. We headed north through hedgerows and tree lines, across open fields, and up and down dry washes.

Echo Company was now also being hit with just about everything the NVA had. They walked into a hornet's nest and were pinned down with automatic weapon fire and mortar rounds. For a moment, I thought I was back on the rifle range in the States where the weapons fire was continuous. From one end of the range to the other, rifle fire was constant.

Grenades and mortar rounds exploded now and then, and some were in front of me. I heard thumping sounds. We were the only ones who made those sounds as if mortar rounds were being dropped in a tube.

We encountered more rows of hedges, then another open field. The firefight was growing intense again, and my heart was beating pretty fast. We tried to be careful going through the hedgerows in case of booby traps.

I kept thinking, "When are we going to get there and help our brothers? Once we get there, can we help them? Can we surprise the enemy?"

We didn't want to waste any time or get caught in a cross fire so we hurried through the shrubs. After about fifteen minutes of fighting the brush just to stay on line, we halted in a wash and waited for the platoon to form up abreast again. We struggled slowly up the side of the wash and sat down on our knees until everyone was out.

I thought we were coming up behind the NVA and would surprise them. If so, we would be able to engage from one of the gullies and be protected by trees. But wishful thinking in Vietnam rarely panned out.

The company commander shouted, "Move out!"

We headed slowly across the open terrain. The firefight was still pretty heavy, and sporadic loud explosions ripped the air. We were still thirty yards from the next tree line when all hell broke loose again.

I heard mortar rounds being dropped one right after another into a tube, "Ploop! Ploop! Ploop!"

This seemed like a different sound than our mortar rounds, but there was so much intense artillery fire that there was no way to know if they were ours or the NVAs. All of a sudden, mortar rounds were falling all around us and exploding. As soon as the first mortar round exploded, machine-gun and small-arms fire opened up from along the tree line and hedgerow. The hedgerow was like dense thickets growing along a creek bank.

Corpus, the Marine from Texas, was about four paces from me on my left flank and another Marine was four paces to my right. Suddenly a tremendous amount of automatic weapon fire came toward us from the front. I heard bullets zooming by me. The initial burst hit my friend Corpus in the chest. He immediately went down and didn't move.

I don't know why I didn't get hit. All I knew was I had to return fire into the hedgerow and tree line ahead of me. Shouts of "Corpsmen!" were going up all around. I ran toward my wounded friend. I emptied one of my rifle magazines into the tree line then grabbed his flak jacket. As I pulled him toward a large dirt mound, my platoon sergeant helped.

"Hold on," I told him. "A corpsman will be here soon."

"Corpsman!"

In seconds, one came running.

"You'll be all right now," I said as I pulled another magazine from my pouch. "Hang in there. You'll be all right."

It was too late. Corpus was gone. I looked down at him before he closed his eyes. He had kind of a faint smile on his face. Ironically, he seemed to go peacefully.

I was devastated. And I was mad. This enemy had inflicted terrible harm on someone I cared about. I knew it was war and that war was hell but I still felt overwhelmed at the loss of my friend. Frustration took over and I wanted to do everything I could to get back at the enemy.

Our platoon was continually hit hard, possibly worse than all of the companies. It seemed like the machine-gun fire was coming from one corner of the hedgerow and tree line so I hurled grenades like baseballs toward that spot. Mortar rounds continued to kick up dirt until it rained soil. There was a lot of shouting.

I automatically returned fire until my M-16 jammed. Clearing it was at least a two-step process and took too long in the field. There was no time to clear my rifle unless I had some cover. So I went right to my next weapon and threw grenades into the hedgerow. Some exploded on impact and some were a little delayed. I wished they would have all exploded immediately.

When my grenades were gone, I pulled the grenades from my friend's pouch and chucked them at another machine gun in the tree line. When those ran out, I cleared the M-16 and resumed fire.

Another one of my team members got caught out in the open when his weapon jammed. Our rifles kept jamming and that made things worse.

As he bent over trying to clear his rifle, I heard the crack of small arms and watched as a round hit him in the stomach. He screamed as he fell.

"Stay down!" I yelled.

I ran the ten yards to his position and checked his wound, all the while firing to give him some cover. A corpsman ran out. As we stood beside the wounded Marine, the corpsman reached into his unit one medical bag. Another burst of small arms fire hit the corpsman in the stomach. He was able to grab his kit and crawl behind some cover.

I stuck with the wounded Marine and returned fire. Then I picked him up by his flak jacket to drag him to safety. The platoon sergeant ran out and grabbed him by his cartridge belt. Together we carried him behind a tree surrounded by shrubbery. The entire time, small arms fire continued coming in on us.

After the Marine was safe, I continued returning fire. The fighting was so intense I reloaded my magazine several times. Things were moving extremely fast. I couldn't say how long the battle lasted but there were times it all seemed to be happening in slow motion. It certainly wasn't going fast enough for me. Small arms fire and mortar rounds were still coming in. A bluish haze filled the air and the smell of death began to rise from the field.

The firefight lagged and kicked up over and over. Then it turned very intense again. Mortar rounds fell from the blue skies and exploded all around us. Bullets whizzed by my head, some kicking up dirt right in front of me. Because the battle was so loud, no one could hear any commands.

One other Marine was still out in the open field hugging the ground and returning fire at the invisible enemy.

"Come back," I hollered, "Get behind some cover!"

Instead, he jumped up and charged the enemy line. He was immediately hit with several rounds of small-arms or machine-gun fire. He fell about twenty yards from the trees.

I yelled out to see if he was alive. I didn't know if he'd even be able to hear me over the explosions that continued to deafen us all. One of his arms wavered in the air before it dropped.

"Hold on," I hollered. "I'll get you!"

Machine-gun fire and mortar rounds were coming in without a break. The smoke got a little heavy, lingering about head high.

I emptied my M-16 into the tree line and had slipped in another magazine when the rifle jammed. I got another rifle, shooting where I thought the enemy was. It seemed like I was the only one firing in the area because my fire team was wounded.

By that time, I was so frustrated I threw the weapon down and ran across the open field. The wounded Marine was nearly thirty yards out and only ten yards from the enemy line. But Marines weren't supposed to leave their dead and wounded behind.

These were my men, my fire team. They were my responsibility and I was going to bring them back—dead or alive. One of the Marines who got hit had just joined our unit. He was from Tulsa, Oklahoma, not too far from my hometown of Konawa.

"Hold on," I told him again, "I'll get you out."

He said something but I couldn't hear what. The incoming mortar rounds exploded all around us.

I kept hearing mortars being dropped down a tube..."Thump! Thump! Thump!" sounds.

Small arms fire kicked up the dirt, but after a brief struggle, I brought the wounded Marine back to cover. There was not time to think. I just had a job to do.

A waiting corpsman immediately started working on him. As he dug through his unit one kit, he asked if I'd been hit or wounded. I had a lot of blood on me. I really don't remember what I told him. I do remember picking up his M-16 to return fire.

There was a specific spot where the NVA machine gun might have been hidden. The weapons fire from the tree lines had subsided a bit. I ran down the line to my right where several wounded Marines were taking shelter and asked if anyone had an M-79 grenade launcher. The M-79 grenade launcher would have taken out that machine gunner in a second but no one had one that was still working.

After checking on their wounds, I told them to take care and ran back to the corpsman. Positioned between the enemy and the wounded Marines, I continued returning fire. Glancing over my right shoulder, I saw that the wounded Marines were being carried to a safe area behind our line. I stayed where I was to provide cover fire.

Finally, the firing stopped.

Every once in a while I'd look up and see jets overhead. Once, I saw a UH-1E Huey gunship and the propeller-type A-1 Sky Raider coming in for close air support. The Huey fired its rockets at the NVA. The Raider came in parallel to our lines but I wasn't sure if it was able to drop bombs on the NVA position or not.

I also heard a Phantom but for some reason, my biggest memory was of the Sky Raider. We were so close to the NVA line, artillery support was out of the question.

Hugging was a common tactic…the enemy stuck so close to the U.S. troops during a fight that artillery and aircraft strikes couldn't be called in. The shells would kill us as quickly as the enemy.

By that time, the wounded Marines were being carried off the field and placed in a washed out draw. A bluish, gray haze covered the field and the smell or mortar and flesh filled the air. It was a terrible smell.

Most of the mortar attacks had died down and hardly anything was coming in, although sporadic small arms fire still cracked. I couldn't tell if they were still shooting at us but I continued to provide cover fire while wounded Marines were carried out.

The firefight actually started around 0830 hours that morning and lasted all afternoon. I can't describe how time passed on that day. Some of the action seemed in slow motion while other times seemed like the whole ordeal zipped by in minutes. I couldn't tell what time it was. I didn't think about being tired or thirsty. I was just doing my job.

It was a miracle I wasn't seriously wounded. It certainly could have happened with me running all over the field, disregarding my own life for the safety of others.

Instinct and prayer got me through.

Soon the CH-34s landed behind us to pick up the dead and wounded.

* * *

Even though my injuries were minor, they either got the best of me or I was flat-out exhausted. I had pulled several wounded Marines to safety, covered quite a lot of ground, and lost track of time. I must have passed out because the next thing I remember was waking up in the washout with other injured and wounded Marines.

Later I was helped to the staging area for the medevac, about a mile from the fighting. I received shrapnel wounds to both legs and a concussion. Shrapnel was flying all over the place from the mortar rounds going off in the area. I barely remember hearing the fighting except for the Huey gunship firing its rockets into the enemy position. They sat me next to another wounded Marine and a corpsman assessed my injuries. He told me to keep an eye on the other guy after he was bandaged up.

The wounded Marine periodically opened his eyes. I always told him he would be all right. I wondered if he was in much pain and tried to comfort him as best I could by telling him we'd be out of there in no time. Several injured Marines were spread out around the area, and some had been placed into fighting holes like the Marine next to me.

Choppers were coming in, picking up the critically wounded, and quickly leaving.

Then the LZ was pounded with incoming mortar and rocket barrages. Marines ran for the nearest shelter and covered the wounded but some got hit by shrapnel. I covered the wounded Marine with my body until the barrage stopped.

More choppers risked coming back. One CH-43 dropped off supplies and reinforcements. Some of those guys looked like brand-new Marines; they still had on their green utility uniforms. Most made it off but a few were hit by either a sniper or small arms fire from the tree line. Those guys went right back into the chopper.

I felt pretty sure the helicopter had itself been hit but they still flew out. Those pilots took big risks and endangered themselves and their crew by coming in to hot LZs. They were brave men and I was thankful for every one of them.

Con Thien was being bombarded with rockets and artillery rounds as we were being hit. I kept hearing the rumbling sounds which only meant incoming. So I hunkered even lower. The rounds landed closer and shrapnel flew everywhere. Between that and the heavy casualties, the medevac took all afternoon.

Marines who were in critical condition or seriously wounded were taken first; the more severely injured were taken to a hospital ship floating off the coast. The less severely injured were flown to D-Med at Dong Ha. It was getting late when a corpsman and his assistant finally removed the Marine from the hole next to me. The corpsman told me I should be next.

As the evening grew late, incoming rounds tapered off and only a handful of wounded were left. The corpsman finally got us aboard a chopper and we flew out with no problems. The next thing I knew we landed at the helipad at Dong Ha where a group of corpsmen stood by to take us to D-Med. It was pretty dark by the time I got in for treatment.

After my condition was assessed, I was told to have a seat. I don't know how long I waited but it seemed like a lifetime before they finally called my name. They did a quick check of my injuries, patched me up, gave me a sling, told me to take it easy, and to return in a few days for a re-evaluation.

I walked through the darkness trying to locate Golf Company. Some Marines pointed the way. I was dog-tired but I managed to walk the distance. When I saw some dim lights inside a tent, I asked if that was Golf Company. They said, "Yeah."

I was so relieved to settle down and rest. I told them who I was and what had happened.

They asked me a lot of questions but I was in no mood to talk. One of the clerks gave me a C ration and told me to find a cot in the last three rows of tents. I dragged my tired, worn-out body to the back corner of one. I sat there in the dark trying to think about what had happened. Everything seemed like a dream.

I was numb and my thoughts seemed to be in slow motion. Except for the memories of what had happened on the battlefield...they were fast.

I couldn't believe I wasn't killed. I started to tremble and my knees shook. I thought about my parents and how they would have handled a notice informing them that their son had died in the Republic of South Vietnam.

I thought about losing my very best friend out there. I wished I could have had the honor of escorting him home but that wouldn't happen. I thought about the Marine who was medevacked out and the

Marine from Oklahoma. I tried to eat but I just wasn't hungry or thirsty. I was too shook up. I couldn't remember when I'd last had anything to eat or drink. During a firefight, Marines think of everything but food and water. Even if I had water, there was no time to drink.

Finally, one of the administration clerks came over and asked me why I was sitting in the dark. He started asking me questions. "We'd been listening on the radio and it sounded like we'd run into hell," he said.

"Yeah," I replied.

He did most of the talking. I tried to answer but got really tired. Maybe I was in shock, I really don't know. I just remember thinking about it and thinking about it, but not wanting to talk.

He told me where the mess hall was then left me alone, again in darkness. I rolled my flak jacket into a pillow and tried to shut off my brain as I lie back. The night sky was perfectly clear and the stars were brilliant. I thought how nice they looked, just like when I was a kid sleeping outside.

It seemed like a lifetime had passed since then. I finally started dozing and before long, I was fast asleep.

Chapter Nineteen

Grave Registration

Nothing in the world is so exhilarating as to be shot without result.
Winston Churchill (Date Unknown)

The next thing I knew sunlight was beaming on the tents. It was extremely bright. I made a head call then stopped by the water buffalo and washed up with cold water. I had to find a towel since I'd left mine, along with other items, in the battalion area before going on patrol.

My first morning at Dong Ha was like those at any military base. Pots and pans were banging in the mess hall, and the strong coffee and bacon smelled really good. All of a sudden I was hungry but I'd left my mess kit in the bush. I stopped by the company office to borrow someone's kit. A Marine said, "Here, take mine. I'll wait until you get back to go to chow."

As I headed for the mess hall, my stomach was growling. I could have eaten everything they offered but I didn't want to pig out. When I finally arrived, I was thankful there were no lines. The servers loaded my mess kit with scrambled eggs, bacon, and S.O.S. Further down the line there were also pancakes, fried potatoes, and French toast with syrup but my mess kit was already full. The extremely important item was coffee.

"Man, that was living!" I thought. "I hadn't eaten like this in a long time."

There were so many items and I got full fast so I had to pass on some of them. I knew to be patient. I would get to it all in the coming days. I was very thankful for the new day and wanted to enjoy my breakfast. The coffee was so good and strong I went back for a second cup.

The setup was totally different than what we had in the bush. I was so used to eating cold C rations the difference was astonishing. It was just like the difference in facilities from boot camp up to active duty in Bremerton, Washington. My first morning at Bremerton, I walked down the stairs from my sleeping quarters and there was the mess hall.

Meals were set up buffet style and they used plates instead of trays. I found a real glass for my milk and a regular mug for my coffee, along with silverware. Several small white tables on one side of the dining area were for the SNCO and non-commissioned officer (NCO). The other tables were long with white tablecloths and small bouquets of artificial flowers. To me, it looked like a fancy restaurant.

I kept thinking, "Is this the way I'm going to live at my first duty station?"

That day in Vietnam, I appreciated everything I had. After washing the mess kit, I headed back to the company area to return it. Then I sat down to write a letter to my parents and cousin who was also stationed somewhere in country. I think he was in Saigon with the Army. Of course, I had to borrow letter-writing gear. When supply opened, I could grab my own items from my Willie Peter, or waterproof bag, including an extra towel.

Then, one of the administration clerks turned to me.

"Grave registration called," he said. "They brought in some of Golf Company's Marines. They need someone to make identifications. Will you do it? They want us over there right away."

I put on my flak jacket and helmet. On the way over, the clerk asked if identifying these guys would bother me.

"I honestly don't know," I said, "but we'll find out."

It was a nice day. The sun was shining and a few clouds were heading north to North Vietnam. At the registration site, a young man met us just inside the door. All he had on was a T-shirt and smock so I wasn't sure if he was Army or Navy.

I don't remember how large the area was because he only took me into one section of the building. Rows of bodies filled the space; so many that I couldn't even begin to guess at their number. There were a lot of units in that area from all branches of the military.

There was a smell in the air that was familiar from the combat I'd experienced. There's no way of describing that smell to where others can really understand. If it's possible to imagine the smell of death, though, that's it. There was also the faint smell of embalming fluid or similar chemicals.

We were led toward litters stacked four high. He stepped on the edge of the litters and unzipped one of the body bags. The clerk knew the first Marine so I just confirmed the identification. In another area, we went through the same process. At the rear, some litters had been placed on a deck. A few of the body bags were just lumped in the middle of the litter.

Again, the bag was unzipped. I knew this Marine. He was one of the newer men who'd arrived the previous month. We finished our identification and the young man thanked us. He also said more men were coming in and that he'd need my help again.

As we made our way toward the company office, the clerk said, "I got a little sick in there from the smell. But I felt better when the cool breeze hits me once we get outside."

I told him it hadn't bothered me. I'd gotten used to death in the bush.

* * *

I'd been in the company area a couple of days when an office clerk came to my tent.

"Your platoon sergeant recommended you for the Navy Cross medal," he said.

Since I still had some ringing in my ears, I thought he'd said the platoon sergeant was getting the Navy Cross.

"If anyone deserves a medal, it'd be the platoon sergeant," I said. "He's a good and faithful leader."

He'd been awarded the Silver Star with Combat V before the firefight on September 21. I thought he also deserved a battlefield promotion. It never occurred to me that I'd be recommended for an award, much less the Navy Cross.

My only thought was that I did what any Marine would in a situation like that.

A clerk from the administration office asked if I was able to travel.

Since my sling had been removed that morning, I told him yes. I just needed to keep exercising my shoulder so it would fully heal.

He asked if I wanted a quota for R&R in Singapore. I said, "Sure!"

I was anxious to get away from the DMZ for a while and relax. I'd only been out of the bush for a few days, so it was probably around the 24th of September. I received a briefing, including how much money I would need. The clerk gave me my orders, sent me to the disbursing office for money, and told me to be in Da Nang by the next evening to manifest for my R&R flight.

I thought, "What a treat!"

*　*　*

I couldn't believe it. Just days ago, I'd been in the bush. Now there I was, getting money for an R&R trip to Singapore. What a relief. The clerk at the disbursing office told me how much money I saved while in country, and I was pleased. I didn't need any of it in Vietnam so I'd saved a lot.

I walked out with $600 in my pocket and felt like a millionaire. I made it back to the company area and started getting cleaned up, all the time hoping and praying we wouldn't have a rocket attack that night. I couldn't wait for morning. I was looking forward to this trip. It would be ten fewer days I had to serve.

I woke up early and headed to chow. I could have survived on coffee alone but since I didn't know what my day would be like, I ate up. I rushed back to gather my gear and headed to the air strip.

"So far, so good," I thought.

The sun was coming out and it looked like a beautiful day but all I could think was, "Please, let me get on the KC-130 and get out of here before we get any incoming."

I stood with other Marines who said they were going south. A plane was sitting on the tarmac with its propellers whirling, and they motioned for us to climb inside.

I thought, "It won't be long now."

Sure enough, as soon as the crew chief came aboard, the pilot turned up the engine and we started down the steel mat runway. We arrived in Da Nang before noon. I still had some ringing in my ears and the noise from the aircraft bothered me so much I was anxious to get off. I was looking forward to enjoying myself, eating a lot, and maybe even having a few beers. I had that same feeling just like I did with my first thirty-day leave after I'd finished training.

After boot camp and the graduation ceremony, orders were issued to all the new Marines. Some had orders for Western Pacific (WESPAC), meaning anywhere west of California. I was lucky; my orders were for Bremerton, Washington, for Marine Security Guard duty. They gave me thirty days of leave plus travel time before the tour started, and I looked forward to spending it with family and friends.

The hard choice was what to do first. Should I see my family right away or visit my former girlfriends? My parents won. The day after graduation, cabs and shuttles lined the streets and the road outside Camp San Mateo. I had on my light summer uniform, the tropical uniform that sported the private first class (PFC) stripes made me so proud.

My National Defense Ribbon was pinned above my left shirt pocket. The ribbon was issued to active duty personnel who'd completed ninety days of active duty. Three stripes ran vertically, two red with a yellow one in the middle. My shoes were all spit-shined, and my hair was getting long enough on top so I could part it.

I looked sharp! I was ready to go home and make my family proud. I caught the shuttle to the Los Angeles airport with several other Marines. When it was time to board, I had a green carry-on bag with a yellow U.S. Marine Corps logo. I felt so good carrying that bag. When anyone talked to me, it was "Yes, sir," or "No, ma'am." The Marine Corps had taught me well.

During the couple of hours on the airplane, I realized I didn't know where any of my relatives lived. I'd never needed to know their addresses before. How was I going to get back home? All I had was the

175

address of my brother. Not one of my relatives had a telephone so I couldn't call anyone to meet me.

As much as I hated to, I called my ex-girlfriend's parents. They said they'd be more than happy to pick me up. They were at the airport in a matter of minutes, and boy, the look they gave me. They were surprised and laughing as we greeted each other. I was quite changed from the last time they'd seen me.

On the way to their house, we talked about all the things I'd missed while in training. When I said, "Yes, sir" and "Yes, ma'am," that got them laughing again because I was so polite. At their house, the missus fixed a home-cooked meal. Then they took me to my brother's house.

My brother gave me a big bear hug. Then he saw my PFC stripes and rubbed them. The next day he and his family took me to Konawa. When we pulled up the driveway, Mom didn't see me until I got out of the car. She quickly walked over and gave me a kiss and started crying. She was very happy to see me, especially in my summer uniform, which was getting wet by then from all the tears.

They said I looked good. That was important to me. You know how families are—they like to fuss over you and Mom cried at everything. When Dad saw me, he moved into the kitchen away from everyone else. He was so overwhelmed he didn't want to start crying in front of everyone. I walked into the kitchen to give him a hug.

"I love you, Dad," I said.

He couldn't hold back any more. He started crying and said, "I love you, too."

"It's good to see you."

I left him alone so he could regain his composure. When all the crying stopped, everyone sat down and talked about what was happening in Konawa. Before long, people started arriving. Although my parents had no telephone, word got out that I was home.

Plans were made for me to come to one home for dinner then another big dinner was planned at someone else's place. After a couple of days, my friends invited me out and I partied a lot on weekends. I believe I put on ten pounds during my stay just from eating and drinking.

When my thirty days were up, I caught the Greyhound to Bremerton, Washington. I was broke, fat, and happy but it'd been worth it. Still, I was glad my leave was ending. While I hated to leave home, I was afraid everything would go back to the same old way again if I didn't leave. Besides, I'd be unauthorized absence status (UA) if I didn't show for my first duty assignment.

I realized then that my home was wherever the Marine Corps sent me. Even when I was on leave in the States, I always had to return to active duty and my Marine brothers. It was no different a world away pulling duty in Vietnam or relaxing in Singapore.

So there I was in Da Nang wondering what I could do to pass the time and still catch my flight the next morning to Singapore. I settled my gear into one of the hardbacks...next to the door, as usual, for a quick exit to the sandbagged bunkers.

I overheard someone say they were going to the PX at Freedom Hill so I asked for directions. Quite a few troops were walking in both directions, some carrying sacks of goodies. I just walked through the PX looking around. It looked every bit like the PX at Camp Pendleton except young Vietnamese girls worked behind the counters.

There were a couple of Caucasian faces. We called them round-eyed girls. Even though I hadn't been gone that long, it was nice to see them. Many Red Cross workers were also in the area, or maybe they were USO girls. Whoever they were with, they were all lovely, attractive young ladies. I wondered why in the world they'd come all the way to Vietnam.

Since I wasn't in the mood to buy anything, I found a theater nearby. The next show started in half an hour so the attendant let me buy my ticket and go in to cool off. I made a beeline for the concession stand and bought a bag of popcorn and a soda. The theater was clean and the air conditioning was humming. It was just like being in the States.

I found a good spot and sank into one of the most comfortable chairs I'd ever felt. I sat there looking dumb and eating popcorn with a couple other early birds who were also avoiding the heat. I couldn't believe I was in a war-torn country getting ready to watch a movie.

When the lights dimmed and the curtains parted, the National Anthem played over the PA. I fought back tears as video clips showed what America stood for. It was so hard to hold myself together I was glad no one was around to see those tears running down my face. A lump in my throat swelled to the size of an apple.

I was so proud to be an American, a Native American Indian at that. There was much in my culture to be proud of. If I were back in Oklahoma, I might have gone to a Stomp Dance instead of a movie. When I was a lot younger I went to them and even made an attempt to get involved.

Stomp Dances were really great social occasions held throughout the Maskokvlke (Muscogee Creek) community. The name Stomp Dance is an English term referring to the shuffle-and-stomp movements. In our native language it is called Opvnkv Haco, which means "spirited" or "high-spirited" dance.

The Stomp Dance started as a way to honor the green corn at the time it starts to ripen. The dance is a renewal of religious beliefs and an opportunity to have fellowship. Everything at those ceremonies has a meaning, even when the men gathered the wood for the fire. The fire was considered sacred and was called many things including Grandfather.

The entire event might start as early as Friday evening with the lighting of a ceremonial fire. The fire stayed lit until the Stomp Dance conclusion on Sunday. Early on Saturday, families set up campsites. They cooked over open pits, just like in the old days. Some people put up tents while others made do with a blanket or tarp and cots or makeshift beds. Some bedded down on the ground.

The ceremony started around 4:00 in the afternoon.

While the veterans or elders were dancing, many of the women stood outside the circle with their shawls on, swaying to the beat. In this way they offered their support to the dancers and honored their efforts. Hundreds of people attended these dances, and I saw people circle the campfire for hours.

It seemed that everyone had something fancy to wear to the dances. Back when I was young, only a handful of men wore the traditional Seminole dress shirt. They had a single color for the background with rickrack designs across the chest. Bright yellow or turquoise ribbons were sewn from the pocket to the shoulder. The ends of the ribbons dangled on the front and back of the shirt. Other men just wore regular Western shirts.

There was always an assortment of headgear. Western hats or even baseball caps were popular. A few men wore roaches, a traditional Northern-style head cover made of deer fur and porcupine hair hand-knotted onto a strip of leather. Feathers were spiked on top so they swayed as the dancers moved.

During the dancing, the Meko or Chief of the Stomp Ground pounded continuously on a handmade drum. It never stopped. I loved to hear the songs and the turtle shells. After the ceremonial dances, supper was served. Just about anyone could walk up to any campsite and be fed. The women took pride in their cooking and made everyone feel like kings by waiting on them.

The actual Stomp Dance began around 10:00. Men led the proceedings with a song or chant. As each individual man joined the circle around the fire, a woman fell in behind him rattling her shells. They alternated like this until the circle was complete and everyone was dancing. It got pretty dirty from the dust being kicked up all night.

No matter where I was, from a rural Oklahoma county to a foreign city, it seemed I always found a reason to be proud of my country. Even at the Stomp Dances, everyone honored the veterans with the gourd dances.

In a theater half a world away, it was a video and our national song that made me proud of America. To defend America was an honor, and hearing the National Anthem again brought that home to me hard.

After that emotional beginning, I settled down and enjoyed every bit of the movie. The flick was "The Good, the Bad, and the Ugly" with Clint Eastwood. I wanted to spend some quiet leisure time away from all the things I'd been through during the past couple of days, and this movie fit the bill.

I would have watched anything but since I enjoyed Clint Eastwood, I was in heaven. A good movie with air conditioning and the comfort of these chairs...that added up to a really good afternoon. For a little while, I felt like I was home. It eased some of the tension and stress.

I walked back and hung around the terminal for a few hours. I met a Marine from the Marine Barracks in Bremerton, Washington, and we talked for a bit. Since I'd been in country, I ran into two Marines I'd met at Bremerton.

"What a small world," I thought. "Seeing him made my day. How lucky could I be?"

Although I'd heard that a good band was playing that night at the Enlisted Club, E-club, I decided to pass. I wanted to stay close to the transit area. Nothing could make me miss my flight. The seven days of R&R might be my only chance to see a different part of the world, let alone to take a break. After having chow at a mess hall, I shot the breeze with some men.

Some were also heading out for a break. A few, very few, were actually headed home. They said rockets had hit the end of the airstrip the night before. No major damage had been done; the rounds had been only for harassment. I hoped we didn't get hit that night. Dark was setting in and quite a few illumination flares lit the perimeter of Da Nang's runway. They said it was routine but to get to the nearest bunker if I heard a siren.

They had a bunker commander, which was something new to me. His job was to get everyone out of the hardbacks when the siren sounded. I guess you could call him a fire watch. Sure enough, late that night a siren sounded and I ran to the door. As soon as we all had crammed into a damp, smelly bunker, the all-clear sounded.

Although I lied down on my cot, I was wide awake. I wondered what could happen next. The flares were still going off, artillery fired in the distance, and people were moving around a lot like something was going on. It turns out they were up because they couldn't sleep either. We were all anxious to get away from there. The ones going home wanted to stay awake all night and sleep on the Freedom Bird.

Those guys were very lucky. I remember wishing I were heading out with them.

Chapter Twenty
R&R

Morning came with no other major incidents. The sun was peeking over the horizon, and the air was damp and cold. As usual, there was a lot of coughing as men woke up. When cigarette smoke drifted through the hardback, I couldn't believe someone was smoking that early.

I rushed to get ready. I needed coffee so I zipped over to the mess hall, ate a quick breakfast, and hurried back. For some reason, time was going very slowly yet I was moving fast. Finally the Singapore flight was announced. We boarded the cattle trucks and were transported to a commercial jetliner with Singapore Airlines.

That jet made for a pretty sight with the flight attendants greeting the men as they boarded. I believe the attendants were Chinese. They were so beautiful they could have passed for models. I sat at a window seat. I was still tired so I thought I'd nap once everyone was on board. Before we took off, the attendants handed out hot washcloths to wipe off the sweat. I guess they didn't want us to get their seats dirty.

I relaxed as we taxied down the runway. As the plane rose, Da Nang looked like a big prison compound with all the barbed wire surrounding it. The jet slowly climbed and circled back over China Beach. I saw the rice paddies I'd first seen six months ago. I wasn't going to miss them during my short vacation.

Then we were over blue waters and I saw nothing but whitecaps on the waves. The flight would take ten to twelve hours. I tried to nap but kept waking up. I thought a lot about my parents, wondering if they'd been notified of my injuries during the recent firefight. If so, I wondered how they'd taken the news, especially Mom.

Mom was the kind of person who worried a lot and always wanted to know more than what people were telling her. She was also very sensitive and emotional. I imagined what would happen, especially if someone in uniform came to the door. My older sister would be there to interpret for her in sign language. She would make sure Mom understood that I was fine.

I also thought a lot about my friend Corpus, the guy who'd been fatally wounded. I wondered if his remains had made it home yet. If I ever got out of Vietnam I would make a personal trip to Corpus Christi to see his parents. I'd explore the area that he loved so much. Then I thought about how his parents might react to me or to what I had to say about their son.

I had way too much time on my hands during that flight. I thought about so many things. A lot of questions raced through my mind. "Why hadn't I been hit during the initial burst of fire? Why had others gone down when I stayed standing? Why hadn't a single bullet found me all that time I was running around assisting wounded Marines? Why hadn't I been hit?"

I kept thinking that maybe the packet the Medicine Man had given me before going to Vietnam had actually worked. I used the tobacco the Medicine Man mixed for me as often as I could. I'd always been able to use it away from other Marines, just like I'd been instructed. I never thought about it much; sometimes I smoked it, sometimes I didn't.

Could it be that the medicine kept me alive, or was the higher power of God watching over me? The belief I had in my training, my medicine, and my faith in God made me feel safe.

Still, it was a miracle that my only injuries were minor shrapnel wounds to my leg, especially considering what I saw at the morgue. Those Marines had been just a few feet away from me on my right and left flanks. Any one of them could have been me. When I'd returned to the rear in Dong Ha, I had counted my blessings over and over.

There were so many what-ifs. "What would my parents do if I were mortally wounded? What church or place of burial would they pick? Did they know the Marine Corps would provide burial detail?"

My thoughts were a lot different than when I'd first talked about joining the military.

I was very young when the idea first came up. As my siblings and I grew up, Mom challenged us to better ourselves. She said one day she and Dad wouldn't be around to take care of us so we needed to learn to do things for ourselves. I was in my early teens and had never really thought about the military.

Mom actually wanted me to join. She always said she'd be proud to tell people I was in the service. All the time I played baseball and worked to build my upper torso to become a better athlete, she always assumed I was preparing for the military. We just fell into this pattern where we joked about it frequently.

I said, "When I get old enough, I'm going to enlist in the military then go away and never come back."

After my little speech, she told everyone in the family, and especially friends, what my intentions were in life. She came up with a new set of charades to get her message across. She imitated a military man carrying a rifle then pointing and shooting things. Mom was a character!

When I was a junior in high school, I moved in with my father's sister and her husband. This was after my folks moved to town and I wanted to stay in Vamoosa High School. During my varsity year, I was the star pitcher with a pretty good win/loss record. My fast ball was crisp and my curve ball kept the batters off their stride. I also was a good right-hand hitter with several homeruns under my belt.

During the summer, I kept my arm in shape by playing independent baseball for my cousin's husband's team in Oklahoma City. All the members were Indians from the community and we traveled around the county playing against other Native teams. One Sunday I pitched my best game ever. I struck out a total of seventeen batters. Needless to say, we won the game 19 to 0.

My baseball mate wanted me to go to Oklahoma City with him to try out for an AA farm team called the 89'ers. The offer was good but I couldn't afford to make the trip. Even when they offered to pay the expenses, I didn't feel right about it. I sometimes wonder where I would be today had I taken that offer.

Partly because of my Mom and partly from decisions I'd made, I ended up serving my country in a foreign land. Every Native American tribe has different values they hold above all others. Things like courage, honor, pride, and devotion to duty were common ones. I believe these traits were reinforced by the military training I received. No matter how my life would have been if I had made other decisions, the path I was on was a good and honorable one. I couldn't have been more proud.

Finally I wore myself out with all that thinking. I dozed off and didn't wake up until the captain told us to fasten our seatbelts for arrival.

* * *

Singapore looked somewhat gloomy; all the thick smog reminded me of Los Angeles. On the river, cargo ships bellowed smoke from their stacks. As we flew over the city, I thought about what I would do first. Enjoying a cold beer and a hamburger were on the top of my list. Hopefully the hotel restaurant had good hamburgers.

I knew I wanted to stay in the first night. I didn't trust anyone I didn't know, especially in Singapore. Even with that cautious approach, I was ready to enjoy myself. We were met on board by a liaison from the R&R center. He gave us a briefing on what to expect and how we were to conduct ourselves.

We headed to a holding area where someone else welcomed us to Singapore. He gave us a breakdown of hotels hosting R&R personnel and told us we could choose any one we wanted. Buses were already waiting for us. When he said to return at a certain time to manifest back to Vietnam, everyone groaned.

"Why did he have to say Vietnam?" one Marine asked.

I didn't let that bother me. I wanted to enjoy myself but I also didn't want to miss muster and be stranded there.

The hotel I chose was a short distance from downtown. Everyone introduced themselves as we headed over. Palm trees lined the streets, and lots of people rode bicycles on the edge of the road. I heard so many automobile horns on the short ride I thought we were in New York City; those folks certainly took advantage of their horns.

The hotel wasn't bad looking. The white building had palm trees at the entrance. The landscape was lush and included plenty of bird of paradise plants. There was even a small pond with a fountain at the center. The entire ground had a deep green, manicured lawn. I wanted to relax and was anxious to get to my room.

After stowing my personal gear, I headed back to the lobby to buy a couple sets of civilian clothes. I didn't want anything fancy, just a change of clothes for the five or six days I'd be there. I bought two pairs of trousers, shirts, some shorts and socks. I didn't need shoes as I brought my dress shoes in my gear.

Back in my room I called for two bottles of cold beer to be sent up. Room service was at the door quick so I was happy. I sipped on one while taking a shower. Believe me, that water was hot. I stayed in there a while, enjoying the fact that no one was telling me to hurry and get out. After that I watched a little television. I didn't understand what the actors were saying but the TV was on and that was all that mattered.

I was just a country boy from Oklahoma, so this was all new to me. I had my own hotel room, something I'd never had before. I was venturing into new territory and exploring the world. I leaned back on the bed and tried to relax among the peace and quiet. My new clothes were laid out in case I decided to go somewhere. Who knew? I might meet someone.

It seemed like there were always opportunities to meet women.

Well, you never know. I was enjoying that second cold beer and the babble of the TV when a knock came at the door. There stood a young woman in her thirties. "I am the hotel hostess," she said. "You would like an escort?"

"Oh, no, thanks," I said. "I'm not going anywhere."

I thought escort meant taking me around town. Now I wonder if she really meant something different. She said to let her know if I changed my mind and left.

I finished my beer and got dressed in case someone else came knocking. Near dark, I decided to head downstairs to find something to eat. A few men from the bus were in the restaurant. I said hello and sat at an empty table.

I asked for a cold beer and ordered a cheeseburger with fries. By the time my order came, the restaurant was filling up. Next door a band was doing a sound check. I decided to go listen.

The area was dim with a spinning globe in the ceiling that reflected sparkling lights. As soon as I sat down, a young girl appeared. "Can I join you?" she asked.

"Sure."

After we introduced ourselves, she asked me to buy her a drink. I thought, "Why not?"

Big mistake!!! Her drink came in a tiny glass with something green stuck in it and a ticket. The waitress said, "Four dollars, please."

"What!" I squawked. "Four bucks for that little thing? My drink only cost a dollar and half!"

Needless to say, I paid for the drink. The girl promptly thanked me and smiled. It turns out the ticket was to keep track of how many drinks she got people to buy. The more she earned for the owner, the more she got paid.

I bought her one more round before telling her I was tired. In the hotel lobby, I bought a mixed pack of miniature liquor bottles and snacks. I stayed in for the rest of the night to avoid spending all my money on drinks.

"Four dollars for a little drink, my eye," I muttered. "That's what I get for being a gentleman."

* * *

Even though there wasn't much to do to get dressed, I took my time getting ready the next morning. I'd never had to shave much, just two whiskers and I was done. I headed downstairs for breakfast. The place was quiet compared to the previous evening. As I walked into the restaurant, a couple of African-American men at a table said, "You have to seat yourself or you can join us. We're on R&R, too."

I sat with them and ordered coffee. They hadn't ordered yet so we had coffee together and introduced ourselves and identified our service branches. Both of them were Air Force stationed at Da Nang. I told them I was a Marine from I Corps stationed at Dong Ha.

Breakfast was about the only thing the cooks there didn't mess up. As we ate, we talked about the previous night's events. "Anyone offer you an escort?" one of the guys asked.

"Yeah," I said. When I described the young lady, he shook his head.

"That sounds like the same woman who approached me. She offered me escort services for five days, $200."

The other guy started laughing. "She'd better be good for that amount of money," he said. "I wouldn't pay anyone to be with me. That lady's just a pimp. I heard they do that here."

I laughed along with them. This was news to me.

"Well," the first man said, "if I'd taken her up on her offer, I would've picked the hostess. She was foxy!"

The other fellow kept saying, "She's a pimp, I'm telling you! A pimp!"

After breakfast, the pair asked me to join them that day. Since I didn't have any specific plans, I agreed. Out front, a group of older men wearing turbans set up a show. They put out round baskets, some of which were big and tall. As we walked up, one of the airmen asked what was in the baskets.

The first old man whipped off the lid and pulled out a huge snake. It was either a boa constrictor or a python; I didn't know the difference. We all jumped and the old guy started laughing. The second man lifted the lid on another basket and began playing a flute. Sure enough, out came a cobra with its hood flared.

We jumped even further back thinking it might be a king cobra. The old man said it wasn't. Before we left, the airmen took pictures of me with the python wrapped around my neck. They said they'd give me a copy before we left Singapore. I offered to pay but they refused to take any money. I told him I'd buy him a drink instead.

One of the guys pulled out a brochure and suggested we go to the Tiger Palm Garden. When we hailed a cab, the driver said it was a nice place to go and that yes, we'd see tigers. The trip took about an hour. The driver dropped us off on top of a hill; collected his fare and left.

There were a lot of elderly people walking around this place. We stopped a few young people for information but all they did was smile. Finally we found someone who appeared to work there and asked about the tigers.

"This is the place to see tigers," she said, "but not real."

Then, in the distance, we saw the fake tigers. They were set up throughout the garden along with ornamental flamingos. It was just a garden to wander through for peace of mind and relaxation.

Needless to say, we were disappointed and had a good laugh that the cab driver hadn't told us the tigers were fake. I personally thought it was a big rip-off. We took a cab back but one of the guys told the driver to drop us off a block from the hotel. He'd found a good place to eat the night before when he'd been with a young lady. "I was pretty high," he said. "Me and my lady stopped at this place where we sat on wooden boxes. She ordered fish with rice and I had fried rice and a beer. When the food came, I asked if she was going to eat the whole fish...you know, as in the head and everything."

"What'd she say?"

"She said yes. She picked out the eyeballs with her chopsticks and ate them," he said, making a disgusting face while telling the story. "It grossed me out so much I fell off the box! I couldn't eat after that."

It was so hilarious we were all laughing out loud.

One of the guys said, "Bet you kissed her goodnight, huh?"

He didn't respond right away. Eventually he looked sheepish and said, "Yeah." We all laughed at him for that, too. He kept saying how she'd freaked him out and how all the vendors and others were laughing at him and thought he was drunk. The woman had told them he was sick because of the food.

We stopped at that place and had a cold beer. After a few hours, we headed back to the hotel on foot. I was disappointed that the snake charmers were gone. I was tired from all the cab rides, especially in the heat and humidity. I decided to head up to my room. I told the guys I'd catch up with them later.

The rest of the trip was typical R&R–eat a little food, have a little drink, enjoy the scenery, and fight off the girls. I really did try to stay away from the women. I'm not cheap; I was just short on cash and didn't want to pay four dollars for a drink. I did enjoy myself, though. I got my hamburger with fries, and later even had a steak dinner.

The trip gave me some time to forget about the fighting. That was the important thing.

Chapter Twenty-one
Dong Ha Bound

God give me strength to face a fact though it slay me.
Thomas Huxley, English biologist (1825-1895)

Time went by fast, and my stay in Singapore came to an end. I packed my belongings the night before so I wouldn't miss my flight. I really couldn't believe I was being so careful; I was headed back to Vietnam and didn't want to miss the flight. Wow! That one made me think.

I had reason to be nervous, though. Getting back from leave before my first duty assignment had been an ordeal. It was just my luck that the Greyhound Bus Company went on strike when I arrived in Tacoma, Washington. Up to that point, everything had been fine. I arrived late at night in an unknown city, short on funds, and was stranded in the bus station.

My orders were to report before a certain time that day. I hadn't realized it would take so long to travel by bus to Washington, much less predict a transportation strike. There was no way to get there on time. I called the Marine barracks. They told me to arrive as quickly as I could, and they showed me as logged in that night since I had called.

So I caught a taxi cab from Tacoma. It was a long ride. Even in the dark, the area looked like a nice place to be stationed. As the taxi cruised around Puget Sound, lights reflected off the water. The homes that dotted the area around the Sound flickered through rows of tall trees. I didn't figure I could catch a taxi or ferry to Vietnam, though. When the bus picked up the Marines at the hotel, I was ready to roll.

In a way, I was glad to be leaving. However, my time in Singapore had made a positive difference in my life. If I hadn't joined the Marine Corps, I never would have had this chance to see the world. Maybe the way I spent my time wasn't the way to best see the world but it had been great for me.

On our way down the ramp to the waiting aircraft, I looked over my shoulder. I knew I might never be back there again. It was quiet on the plane; no one was talking, and most of the men were probably tired. As the aircraft made a wide circle over the city, I was amazed at how big the place was. Large cargo ships were docked side by side near a pier in an industrial area stacked with huge containers in every color.

As the plane drifted into clouds, I lost sight of everything. I didn't get much rest listening to all the chatter that suddenly kicked up. The men exchanged stories about the girls they'd met; some of the servicemen were trying to outdo each other and were calling each other liars but it was all in fun.

The entire time, I hadn't thought about Vietnam or what had happened just the week before. I guess time does heal. After about an hour, the plane got quiet again.

My mind drifted back to the September 21 firefight. I wondered again how I'd survived that day. In an instant, with a single bullet or mortar round, I wouldn't be in that seat enjoying the laughter of the other men. A lump stayed in my throat almost the entire trip.

The flight was long. I kept thinking about the things that had happened–mostly what-if questions. "Had we used our 60-mm mortars on the NVA that day? Why hadn't I been hit with all that automatic weapon fire? What if that had been me lying injured out in front of the line. Would anyone have seen me and dragged me to cover?"

The thoughts just kept coming back. I couldn't get that day out of my mind. I remembered the medevac pilots who'd put themselves in extraordinary danger. If not for them, many wounded Marines wouldn't have survived. I could still see those choppers coming in while others circled and tried to land. What a horrible day for Second Battalion, Fourth Marines, and especially for Golf Company.

I thought about one old Marine I'd met who'd gotten out of the Corps some years before. He'd decided to come back because his baby brother had been stationed in Vietnam. He strongly believed that if he returned to the Corps and requested a tour of Vietnam, his brother would be transferred back to the states.

He'd fought hard to get into the Corps because of his age. He'd worked even harder to meet the same physical demands made on younger recruits. He came out of boot camp with his PFC stripes and later received lance corporal stripes. He always joked that some of the young recruits could have been his sons. The DIs always yelled, "Don't let the old man beat you!"

The DIs really challenged his endurance, pushing him through training and making him lose weight. The troops called him Pappy. His brother was down south with the First Marine Division. I often wondered if his brother made it out of Vietnam.

I thought about my friend Corpus, and how we'd never again sit around and tell jokes. I could see him and hear him talking and laughing. And while I could still picture him alive, I also saw him dying on the battlefield.

We'd had some great times together. Even today, I think about him often and get emotional. Somehow, even now it still seems like a dream.

Finally I was able to sleep on the flight. I woke to an announcement that we would be landing in Vietnam soon.

"Oh, no," I said.

I think everyone on the aircraft felt the same way.

Out the window were the same old things—rice paddies and dark green vegetation. Some of the paddies were murky, apparently because they'd been plowed recently. The landing gear clunked as the wheels went down. The R&R had flown past. It seemed like I'd left the day before yet there I was, back already. I wondered what Golf Company was up to and if they'd been pulled back to Dong Ha for regrouping after that day.

Whatever challenges lay ahead, I would get on with my life back home with the rest of Golf Company.

* * *

It was mid-afternoon when we arrived at the Da Nang airbase. Before we even got off the aircraft, people were complaining again. That hot sun hit us hard and the air was very muggy. When our transportation arrived and I saw those wire-screened windows again, I thought how glad I'd be back in the States when I wouldn't have to ride in something like that again.

The cattle trucks were better than nothing but I sure was tired of them. The complaining continued even after we boarded the trucks; it was too hot, there was no air conditioning, we were going too fast or too slow, we were hitting bumps. You name it, there was a complaint.

The concern was actually that we were back in Vietnam but the feelings came out in all those little complaints. Once we got to the terminal, I saw a lot of people inside—new men coming in country and some leaving for home. My flight to Dong Ha would go out the next day. I headed to the transit area and found a cot.

Someone told me to get C rations from the hardback. I grabbed two boxes, one for evening meal and one for morning chow. I picked something simple I could eat cold. That was how tired I was. Some men had a long ration, a meal in a pouch that was dropped into boiling water to heat. The problem was they didn't have a way to boil water so they ate it straight from the pouch.

When I lied down to rest, I listened to the crowd. Somewhere a radio blared out old songs I hadn't heard in a long time. Da Nang was still the same; the artillery rounds were still being fired, hoping we didn't get any incoming rockets. I sure wasn't in the mood to jump into a bunker in the middle of the night.

I couldn't say I was glad to be back in 'Nam but I had a job to do. I would do what they needed me to. I stayed close to the transit area so as not to miss my flight. I didn't realize how late it had gotten until I noticed it was quiet and dark outside. There weren't any rocket attacks that night but there were a lot of outgoing rounds. They sounded like 81-mm mortars, and I heard them hitting the bottom of the tubes— plump, plump, plump.

Illumination flares went up around the air base and the streams from the flares caused the sky to be smoky. I thought there must have been some enemy movement to have all those flares going off. When the siren sounded, I ran to the bunkers. I wasn't in a deep sleep and the sirens really startled me. I sat there trembling, not knowing if it was because of the cold night air or whether I was getting jumpy.

I couldn't wait for the sun to come up so I could head north. I'm not sure why I wanted that; it was actually more dangerous in Dong Ha.

* * *

Morning came and the sun peeked over the horizon. Everyone in the transit area was listening to a radio. The DJ said, "Good morning, Vietnam!" I don't know if it was the real guy who was famous for that saying or if someone was impersonating him. He was playing music, though, and that sounded good to me.

As luck would have it, I was able to leave earlier than scheduled. They called my name, and I headed for the cattle truck that would take me to my flight. I couldn't believe I was headed north again to Dong Ha to be with my company in the DMZ. After boarding the C-130, the aircraft shot almost straight up. I tried to get comfortable but that was nearly impossible on those web seats. I was strapped in and the seats were so low my knees were level with my chin.

A lot of Marines still wearing their stateside utility dungarees were on the flight and they sat there dazed. I was sure they were wondering what was in store for them during the coming year. I'd had that same look when I first arrived. I hoped and prayed we all would make it back home.

We came down pretty fast in Dong Ha. We were hurried out before the NVA could zero in on the airfield.

Although it seemed like it had been forever since the September 21 firefight, only two weeks had passed. It was now October 4, 1967.

It was extremely hot and humid as I walked back toward the company area. Dirt flew everywhere because of the aircraft. As I walked up the road, I looked around the compound. I was amazed at all the things I'd missed seeing my first time at the airfield; either that or they'd put up more tents while I was on R&R.

A clerk said they wanted me ready to go back to the field in a couple of days and that I'd take the company mail. I told him I'd be ready as long as I could get some 782 gear and another rifle. Once I hit the mail room, I was so excited. I received a lot of mail and rushed back to my tent to decide which letters to read first. I guess it didn't matter which ones I read first because I was going to read them all. But I wanted to answer the letters before it got too dark.

I had just finished reading the second when I realized it was time for evening chow. I grabbed a quick bite and rushed back to my reading. I managed to get through only one more letter before a Marine came to talk about the firefight of September 21. He wanted to know everything. He also told me he was sorry he hadn't participated because he really wanted to see some action.

The next morning someone from the admin office told me he'd seen a medal recommendation for me from the platoon sergeant. But the recommendation had been trashed because the senior staff NCO felt I'd only done my job and that didn't warrant a medal.

"Oh, well, I guess he knows what he's doing," I replied.

I couldn't tell if that Marine was pulling my leg or not but I didn't ask for details. The last thing I was going to do was challenge the senior staff NCO's authority. I tried to put it out of my mind and gathered a new set of 782 gear from supply.

That meant filing a missing gear statement. When the supply clerk learned I'd also lost my rifle, he said the armory would want a statement.

I had a new towel to hang around my neck, M-16 rounds in my magazines, insect repellent, and all the other necessities. I was ready to accept the challenge again. It was now close to October 7. In ten more days, I would celebrate my twenty-second birthday in the bush near the DMZ. I thought, "What a celebration that would be."

That evening was a long one. I wondered who was left in the platoon and company, where they were located, who was acting as platoon sergeant, and who the squad leaders were. I tried to write another letter because writing seemed to ease my mind. Picturing myself with family and friends as I wrote them reassured me that I would return home safe and sound.

As I lie on my flak jacket with my helmet as a pillow, I thought about what the clerk said regarding the NCO's decision. It would have been nice if the Navy Cross recommendation really had been for me. It would have been great to go home with that medal on my chest. I even heard a Navy Cross could be upgraded to the Medal of Honor, depending on the circumstances.

Getting the Navy Cross, and especially the Medal of Honor, would be special for any Marine. It would make my parents even more proud of me. My brothers would be equally proud. I kept thinking how special the recommendation would be for me, a young Seminole/Creek man from a small town in Oklahoma. I finally put these thoughts out of my mind and didn't think about it again after that night.

* * *

Morning came quickly. As the sun rose over the horizon, it looked like a normal, nice October day. Eggs, S.O.S., and a cup of strong coffee made for a good, hot meal before I left for the bush. Down at the helipad I joined other Marines going out to join the Battalion.

When we got the wave to board, I ran to the chopper as quickly as possible. We wanted to get off the pad before we got hit with rockets. In minutes, we headed over Highway 9 to the re-supply line by C-2 then into the boonies where the firefight had taken place. Despite going through the horrific firefight a couple of weeks ago, I found myself looking forward to being with my squad, my company. I was anxious to get back to work and continue my job.

Chapter Twenty-two
Rejoining the Company

The CH-46 landed in a clearing surrounded by shrubbery. The Marine directing the chopper indicated where Golf Company might be. I headed toward my battalion, less than two miles from Con Thien, which was still getting shelled by rocket and artillery rounds. The sound of explosions was continuous.

I didn't recognize anyone from the company or platoon. However, the first person to recognize me was an African-American Marine from the weapons section; he and I did a lot of patrols together. Then a handful of Marines showed up to greet me. It was great seeing some of the guys again. I wished the entire platoon could have been there. But I would endure the loss of my friend and be thankful to be with the survivors, no matter how few.

One of the gunners said our company had a lot of new faces. We even had a second lieutenant assigned as platoon commander. The first second lieutenant had lasted only a month; he was medevacked out after stepping on a booby trap. We hardly got to know him before he was gone.

A Marine from the rocket section said we were headed back to Dong Ha soon.

Since I had just come from there, I said, "If I'd known that, I would have stayed back in the company area and waited for you to show up!"

We all laughed and they went back to their fighting holes.

I found the lieutenant and introduced myself.

"Glad to meet you," he said. "I've heard good things about you. Now, I'm short on experienced personnel around here. I want you to be a squad leader."

A squad leader was responsible for all members of his squad. Usually that was about fourteen men but in combat, we averaged about eight. The squad leader reported to the platoon sergeant and the commander to receive instructions and other pertinent information. He would then pass on the information and direct the fire team leaders so they could carry out the orders.

"Okay," I said, "that's fine with me. I'll get my squad together to introduce myself and gather their personal information for my book."

I was assigned to First Squad.

When the lieutenant said we were going back to Dong Ha, probably within a couple of days, I considered that good news. I really didn't want to stay in the field too long. I got used to sleeping in just a little longer, going to chow, and being able to relieve myself without being shot at or having artillery rounds coming in.

Now I had to refocus my attention on the new men under my charge. It was different. I was used to seeing the men I'd already spent quite some time with. Now I had new Marines. I didn't mind; I felt like a mother hen protecting her brood. The men were attentive, alert, and eager to learn from what this seasoned nearly twenty-two-year-old had to say about survival in the bush.

That eagerness would help them learn quickly. I knew they'd be proud one day to help someone else on their first days in country. I'd felt just as eager the day I'd graduated from boot camp. When the band played the Marine Corps hymn, a lump formed in my throat and chill bumps came out all over my body. When the band finished playing, the DIs yelled out our platoon number and said, "Dismissed."

We all took one step back and said, "Aye, aye, sir." Then we did an about face and yelled. We all made it except one private who'd gotten so sick he'd dropped out. That day was one of the proudest moments of my life. I'd achieved something that not everyone could accomplish. I'd become part of the United States Marine Corps. I was one of those "Proud and the Few."

It was a terrific honor to graduate. Now, I considered it just as great an honor to help these new men survive the war. We got orders to work our way toward a washed-out bridge and provide security. Even with the new Marines, we were still way below strength. The battalion ran a few company patrols as we worked our way back home toward C-2.

After a couple of days at the same location, we got up early one morning and headed toward the bridge. As we cleared the thickets, we came upon a main supply route to Con Thein. The area was wide and cleared all around. We thought there might be snipers in the tree line. I found myself thinking of what happened the last time I'd seen a tree line.

We spaced out and the platoon made it across without incident. I thanked God for that. We reached the bridge in the afternoon. The company set up on the northwest corner of the battalion perimeter facing the DMZ. First Platoon was spread out nearby in an overgrown rice paddy, and a handful of Marines guarded the edge of the supply route.

The first fighting hole for First Platoon was about ten feet from the tree line. That made me uncomfortable. The Marines there were well within grenade range. The spot next to it was a two-man hole with a pair of riflemen. Next to that was the M-60 machine-gun team overlooking the rice paddies facing the DMZ. They had a great range of fire across that route.

The M-60 was a specialized weapon handled by a gun squad rather than regular infantrymen. The weapon could blanket an area in bullets but the team had to be careful not to let the barrel get too hot. Otherwise it would melt. A quick-change release latch was rigged so the barrel could be replaced easily. During combat, this had to be done very quickly so they could resume firing as soon as possible.

Next to the machine-gun team was another two-man hole with a couple riflemen. We were spaced out from each other, and as squad leader, I was positioned behind the right rear of the gun crew between them and one of the two-man holes. In other words, I was centrally located with the lieutenant's hole.

For some reason, the lieutenant had been called to the company CP for radio watch. That left his fighting hole vacant. I sat with a radio man in a hole big enough for two. Since we were together, we also shared the radio watch.

In the afternoon, we received word that hot chow would be delivered. That really lifted our spirits. Since we were at a 50 percent alert status, we took turns cleaning our weapons. By having men alternate, some weapons were always ready. The M-60 crew striped down their gun and gave it a good cleaning then stashed the 7.62-mm rounds nearby. They were always ready for action and could be counted on if things got out of hand.

Late that afternoon, the CH43s came in. The mess men carried green vacs and steel containers of coffee and juice off the choppers. When we heard they'd brought steak, morale tripled. The troops went through the line quickly, got their food then headed back to their fighting holes. Creamed corn, salad, and bread were served along with the steak. I wasn't wild about the salad but everything else sounded great.

The knives in our mess kits were so dull they could barely cut the steaks. The meat was tough enough that some of the troops ate with their hands. I was one of them. It was a hot meal and that's what counted most. Everyone was in a good mood because we were headed in the next day. That meant cold beer, soda, and mail. Our weapons were clean, we'd eaten hot chow, and there it was, Friday the 13th.

I was always a little leery when they brought hot chow into the bush. Maybe it was a premonition but the entire time I'd been in Vietnam, each time hot chow showed up, something happened. I kept my fingers crossed that nothing would happen that evening. All of us were anxious for the night to end so we could head back to C-2.

The Marine from the rocket section kept teasing me. He said I should stand hole watch with him and his assistant since we were going in the next day.

"I'll let you write to my sister in Florida as a pen pal," he said, "and I can write to your sister!"

I told him that although I liked standing watch with him, I had to stand radio watch that night.

Our spirits were so high the men joked back and forth all evening. It was getting late when the lieutenant came back just long enough to have me send out an ambush patrol. I gave the squad the password. I also made sure they had a green flare in case they had to come back in. Their instructions were to leave through the front of the line between holes and to come back the same way.

They headed toward the edge of the rice paddy. Because tall trees stood to our left, it was extremely dark at the northwest section of the perimeter. It was also very quiet that evening, so quiet you could have heard a pin drop, but the radio was always busy with chatter. Sitting in our fighting holes wearing our flak jackets and helmets, we waited out the night.

A few illumination flares went off near Con Thein. Flares were always going off because the NVA probed the perimeter at night. They had a hellish day with all the artillery rounds, and I was hoping we could get through this night without anyone probing our lines.

Close to 0100 hours I heard a firefight on the battalion line to our far left—almost behind me. On the other side of the CP, illumination flares were being fired from the 81-mm mortar section. The canisters whistled through the air and made whooping sounds as they hit the ground. Then more chatter came across the radio.

Not long after that, we received a tremendous amount of mortar barrage. Rounds landed everywhere inside our perimeter. Then an RPG slammed into one of the holes to my left. My men were there, the ones near the tree line. It must have been a white phosphorous round, a chemical widely known in the military as Willy Peter, because of the white smoke drifting over from that side of the perimeter.

After that, all hell broke loose. The men opened fire with everything they had. The M-60 machine gun was spitting red fire, and men were yelling, "They're coming in!" The M-60 was doing a hell of a lot of firing. I wondered when it was going to slow down. It amazed me what that team had to endure when the barrel needed to be changed.

I don't know if they ever made that change or if the barrel eventually melted. The gun hole fell silent but the men were still yelling. I could only guess they were in hand-to-hand combat trying to repel the NVA. Some of the crew was armed with pistols and single shots were fired. Suddenly, they were silent.

We continued firing at the invaders inside the perimeter. Every Marine did his part to push the NVA back toward the rice paddy. Chincoms and grenades were being tossed inside and outside the perimeter, and explosions blasted everywhere after the mortar fire lifted.

Some were so loud I knew the NVA was throwing satchel charges inside the lines and into fighting holes. It was a wonder the NVA didn't throw a grenade or a satchel charge in our hole. The smoke was so thick, though, the they might not have seen us despite our hole being out in the open.

Even with the illumination flares, I couldn't see one foot beyond the hole. But I could hear a lot of foot movement inside the perimeter. All the running sounded like a stampede of water buffalos. The radio man and I fired at anyone moving inside the perimeter, hoping the targets weren't one of our own.

A radio call ordered us to tell the Marines to call out the names of the states. By noting which holes responded, we could locate the breach. Meanwhile, my ambush patrol was still out. I wondered how and when I could bring them back safely, either during the firefight or later. I advised them to return along a certain hole and to make sure they used their green star cluster flare.

It was early morning by then. Smoke and the smell of death filled the air. The fighting was so intense that time didn't matter; we just kept fighting. Finally Puff showed up. It let loose with the mini-guns to my left, near the battalion area. Just then the ambush patrol popped their green star cluster. They rejoined their fighting holes, which helped shore up our defensive position. A lull came, and Puff fired away at the NVA somewhere down the battalion line.

Flare canisters whirled through the thick smoke and made thumping sounds as they landed. I didn't know if the illumination rounds were from our 81-mm mortars or the artillery at C-2. We just sat in our holes listening for when the enemy made another assault.

They didn't return. In that long, long hour of waiting, my radio man said, "I'm scared."

"Don't feel bad," I said. "I am, too. But we still have enough ammo left between us. We'll be okay. We'll make it."

Everyone was scared that morning. Some of us beat the odds and fought back the NVA. We were a handful of courageous Marines determined to fight to the end.

* * *

The smoke lingered for a long time. Dawn came over the trees to my right as I stuck my head out of the hole. Puff was still circling the perimeter but as soon as the light grew stronger, it left. I sent a patrol out for a body count. Meanwhile, the men made an assessment of the platoon line.

The news was grim. Eight good Marines had been lost.

The patrol yelled that there were quite a few enemy bodies with no apparent survivors. Then came more shooting. When a member of the NVA moved, one of the patrols shot him. Once the body count was tallied, the patrol gave me a briefing. It looked like the enemy had dragged off some of their dead and wounded because there was a lot of blood on the trail leading into the rice paddy.

The M-60 gun position had put up a good fight. NVA bodies lay in the fighting hole with the Marines. The corpsman said they'd been shot then picked to death with meat hooks. A meat hook lay by the hole and another was still in a Marine.

I thought, "I hope they were dead before being picked with those hooks."

That they had died was bad enough. I hoped they hadn't suffered, as well.

Those men put up a courageous fight. Without them firing away that morning, a lot more of us would have died. They deserved a medal. The brunt of the assault must have fallen on them. The NVA clearly didn't know where our other fighting holes were but the sound of the M-60 was easy to pick out.

The fighting hole I had worried about, the one near the tree line had been completely destroyed. The NVA had shot an RPG into that one. I don't think those men knew what had hit them; their bodies were still smoldering from the white phosphorus.

The Marine from Florida, the one who'd wanted me to stand watch with him, lie in that hole. I couldn't believe I'd been spared. If I had spent the night with them, I would have been one of the causalities. Knowing how many Marines had been lost and that I'd almost been one of them hit me very hard.

I heard a helicopter in the distance. By this time, it was around 0900 or 1000. As dust and debris flew everywhere, the Huey landed behind First Platoon's perimeter. Officers jumped out. It was a general and a full bird colonel, probably from the Third Marine Division Headquarters.

They looked around and came toward my fighting hole. I was getting up to greet them when the General said, "Take it easy. You had a rough night."

"We lost eight Marines, sir," I said. "The NVA overran our gun position but we held our own."

"That was good work. I'm sorry about the lost men." He headed toward our company CP with the colonel following behind.

After the officers made their assessment, they departed. Later, my platoon leader arrived. I don't know where he'd been during the ordeal but he said he was going to be acting CO until a new one arrived. The company CP had been wiped out. After being briefed, the lieutenant said he had to get back. He sure left the area in a hurry.

We were all dog-tired so I told the men to rest until word came down for us to saddle up. I made some strong coffee as I watched the corpsmen doing what they had to do with the wounded and dead. I was proud of those two. They put themselves in harm's way every time they went into the line of fire to assist a downed Marine.

When my coffee was hot, I mixed in the cocoa, cream, and sugar. I really didn't feel like eating. I was sick at the thought of those eight Marines and how they'd died. The corpsmen said they would stay behind until a medevac arrived.

I still had some ringing in my ears from the incoming barrage of mortars. I could only hope it would go away soon. My memories of that day, though, would stay with me forever.

* * *

We didn't say much as we marched up the incline from the bridge area. I glanced over my shoulder for one last look and hoped I never had to go back there again. It had been bad enough going through the September 21 firefight and losing friends there but now this, less than a month later. I wondered who else would be next–was my time coming?

I tried to think about positive things. My men depended on me for guidance and leadership. We were spread out quite a bit, maybe twenty paces or so, in case the NVA spotters called in artillery again. When we crested the hill, the front gate of C-2 stood in the distance. I wished the men could hurry. I prayed nothing would happen to us. I didn't want to see any more casualties that day.

The Marines ahead of the column were already moving into the compound.

I kept thinking, "In another five more minutes, I'll be safe."

Those last five minutes seemed to last an hour but finally I walked through the gate. What a relief! We strung around toward our old fighting holes on the east, and I jumped into the trench and worked my way toward my old bunker. By now my field pack was light because I only had a couple of C rations left.

The afternoon was getting late so I walked around to check on the squad position and the men. I also wanted to check the fighting holes to make sure the squad had their principle direction of fire set up. We sat around shooting the breeze about what we'd done and guessing at what might be next. The seasoned Marines asked if we thought the 2/4 would be pulled back to regroup like last time. I told them I didn't know.

Around dark, I headed back to my fighting hole. It was positioned up front near the road to Con Thien. That evening, an M48 tank parked next to my bunker. I felt somewhat safe with all that firepower but those tankers made a lot of noise. I was told it was because of their starlight scope. I thought it was the turret being traversed around. Either way, it hummed all night long.

We stayed in for a couple more days cleaning our weapons and getting re-supplied. I wondered where we were going but then I thought that it didn't matter. Whatever we had to do, we had to do.

Sure enough, the next morning we saddled up and headed northwest into the bush. It was an all-day affair. It seemed like we just got into the thicket and were setting up for the night when mortar fire came from our left. Our artillery battery opened fire from C-2. I thought it was just a routine fire mission because I heard them all the time.

Our platoon was inside a huge bomb crater facing the DMZ when a firefight broke out to the left. It was fairly late but we still had some light. The next thing I knew we were on high alert because the NVA was probing the lines again. The company to our left took some casualties and the medevac choppers were called in right away.

We hunkered down and stayed ready. My magazine rounds sat next to me for a quick reload. A couple of medevac helicopters came in but I couldn't tell if they landed or not. They traveled over the ridge so I couldn't see them.

Another helicopter came around but this one was hit. With black smoke streaming behind, it banked to the left and went over the ridge. Thick smoke rose up and I couldn't see if the chopper crashed or landed.

After that, a lot of choppers flew around trying to land. One Army medevac with the Red Cross logo came in fast and extremely low. The pilot had a lot of guts and was determined to pick up the wounded Marines even though the LZ was hot. I don't know if he was successful because he disappeared over the ridge like everyone else.

We were on 100 percent alert the entire night, which meant no sleep for anyone. The next morning we saddled up and headed back to C-2 for regrouping.

* * *

We'd been at C-2 for a couple days when I received a call to pick up some new men at the CP. They looked pretty scared. They also needed some sun to tan them up, a lot of sun. I wanted to laugh but held it in. I wondered if I looked like these Marines when I'd first arrived in country.

I sure hoped I didn't. They had nice, clean equipment; their M-16s glistened, and their jungle fatigues were brand new without a spot of dirt on them. I introduced myself and welcomed them to First Platoon,

Golf Company, and to Vietnam. As we headed to the east side of the trench line, I told them to keep a low profile and pointed toward the DMZ.

As we maneuvered over to the platoon sector, I checked my green book to see who was short of men and who would be rotating out for the squad and the platoon. The new Marines kept calling me sir. I told them I wasn't an officer, just a corporal. Finally, they were all assigned.

Back in my bunker, I made coffee and relaxed. It was near the latter part of October. I had celebrated my birthday out in the bush with the bang and fireworks provided by the NVA.

Chapter Twenty-three
The Farewell

Everyone is necessarily the hero of his own life story.
John Barth, American author (date unknown)

I was called again to take a squad of men and a gun crew out on a night patrol. We were to sit in as a listening post not far from C-2's south entrance. I gathered the men to explain the checkpoints for our route. Quite a few new Marines were in the group. I told them I didn't want to hear any rattling and to paint their glasses with camouflage to cut down on any glare that might give away our position.

I explained to the new men that this was a dangerous assignment. We were dealing with NVA troops, and we could run into a company or a battalion. They needed to listen very carefully to my commands. Before we headed out, I checked their paint and had them jump around. There were a few noises but nothing bad.

My radio man checked with the company and battalion CP operators, and made sure we had a spare battery. I verified that our on-call fire support would be available at the checkpoints. Our checkpoints were plotted on the maps of the artillery battery and the 81-mm mortar crew. I didn't want friendly fire wiping us out, nor did I want to end up stranded without fire support and illumination flares.

As it got dark, we moved out through the barbed wire fence and headed south. Our route ran adjacent to the main supply road running up to Cam Lo. We were in thick brush and moved slowly. We had all night, and I didn't want to rush into a dangerous situation and get us wiped out.

About thirty minutes into the patrol, we heard some cattle on the road. The bells around their necks clinked and the animals mooed. It sounded like they were moving toward Cam Lo. Sometimes the enemy used diversions to sneak around at night, and driving cattle was one way to cover their movements.

We sat still and listened to be sure it was only cattle. I sure didn't want to call a fire mission on a herd of cattle and make the villagers mad at us. As the animals headed south, the clinking faded. We waited for some time before moving out again.

Once we found the first checkpoint, we radioed the CP. We also told them about the cattle before heading to the second checkpoint.

All during our movements, flares were going off in the distance. We had to make sure we didn't get caught in open terrain and possibly be spotted by the NVA. Whenever a flare went off, we got down as low as possible and froze. We didn't move until the flare went out.

We made it to all the checkpoints without incident. The remainder of the night, we stayed at the last checkpoint a couple hundred yards from the compound. We were hidden in the thicket, and I staged the men facing away from the compound. The M-60 gun team took a good portion of the open area so they'd have a wide field of fire.

Everything was going okay until early that morning. A gun team member crawled over and told me that one of the new Marines had moved out in front of his crew to take a crap. It smelled up the entire area. Needless to say, I found out which Marine it was and chewed his butt for moving. He could have given away our position.

He apologized but said he couldn't help it. He had a bad case of diarrhea and had to go somewhere. Everyone picked up their belongings and we moved to a new location away from that smelly mess. I didn't want to jeopardize our position any more than necessary.

Daylight came without any more "crap" from the Marine. I was very thankful that we'd made it through the night.

* * *

The next morning, a young lieutenant approached me with a gunnery sergeant who'd just joined Golf Company. The lieutenant was a young Caucasian, slender and not terribly tall. The gunnery sergeant was Hispanic. He was of medium build, wore glasses, and was about average height.

"Can we talk to you in private," they asked quietly, "away from the men?"

Once we were alone, the gunny didn't hesitate with what he had to say.

"I went from recruiting duty to staging battalions," he said. "I've been out of the element too long to be a good leader. I'm not afraid to tell you I'm not proficient in combat. I wouldn't know what to do if a situation came up."

The lieutenant added his own story. "I just arrived, straight from Officer Candidate School. I have no combat experience. Because you're a seasoned NCO leader, I want to offer you a battlefield commission."

He didn't wait for me to respond; he just kept talking.

"If you stay with the platoon and take this offer," he said, "I'll recommend you for second lieutenant. There'll even be a medal to go along with the promotion. I don't think I'll have trouble getting approval and you won't have to go through OCS. The promotion will be effective immediately."

I was pretty much in shock. My knees trembled and I had goose bumps. It was an honor to be thought of so highly by superiors but I was tongue-tied.

I finally managed to say, "I need to sleep on it."

"It is quite sudden," they both agreed, "but we've already talked to the higher authorities in Golf Company. We'll check back with you tomorrow."

I couldn't think straight the rest of the day.

All the nervousness and excitement was overwhelming. I felt like a kid again, like when I'd graduated from high school. Because I'd left school for a while to work, I was twenty years old when I finished. I really felt good about myself. For once in my life, I'd accomplished something.

I'd also been the first person in my family to receive a diploma. Even today, I am the only member of my family to have graduated high school. On graduation morning, my stomach was full of butterflies. It seemed like the hours dragged by and the clock stopped ticking. The ceremony was scheduled to start at 7:30 that evening.

When I got a ride to the school, my classmate asked if I was nervous. He said it would be over before we knew it. We laughed a lot the entire ride. In the school parking lot, we posed for pictures for someone's parents then hurried inside. Finally, we were all lined up for our entrance.

The music began playing. Pomp and Circumstance was the most wonderful sound to my ears. It was a great feeling to put on the cap and gown then walk down the aisle after more than twelve years of hard work. Receiving that diploma was the thrill of a lifetime.

It was particularly special since I'd dropped out for a time. My cousins had left school and taken jobs in the city. I didn't want to miss out on all the fun so I left school, too. My older cousin and I cruised the streets looking for girls and making catcalls. We had clean, wholesome fun like chasing girls and having a good time at the sock hops.

We also went to a number of powwows in the city and outlying areas. Powwows were a different type of dance all together. Dancers came from all over the country. The Western and Plains Indian tribes dominated these events with their colorful regalia.

The program usually started off with a Grand Entry. All the different dancers lined up by category. The traditional men came first with their large feather bustles and bells. The fancy dancers were next, often dressed in bright colors. The ladies in their traditional buckskin dresses led the women, followed by dancers wearing cloth tear dresses.

At the head of the procession, the honor guard carried in the American flag and an eagle staff. After the colors were posted, a flag song was performed.

Veterans from all branches and tribes would perform the Gourd Dance. Only veterans could participate. The men lined up facing the drum. Each had a rattle made either from a gourd or a milk can filled with pebbles or corn. They danced in place to honor all war veterans and those who had passed on during different conflicts.

The powwows in Oklahoma were incredible to watch. Feathers would fly everywhere as the fancy dancers swirled and the grass dancers dropped to their knees. The lady shawl dancers spun around, too, while the jingle dress dancers had their own fancy footwork. Everyone stopped on a dime with the last drumbeat. The dancers were pretty competitive because many of the programs awarded cash prizes.

The last dance was usually called the 49'er. Everyone got into the ring and danced throughout the night. Just like with the Stomp Dances, things didn't break up until dawn.

Needless to say, partying and working for minimum wages got old after a while. I ultimately decided to get a job. Many times I thought about joining the military just to learn a trade. My plan was to get out of the service and get work with the skills the military taught me. That was in 1965.

My brother told me the Marine Corps had been a pretty tough branch when he'd joined back in his glory days of the 1950s. My brother rarely spoke about his time in the service but he was stationed at Twenty-nine Palms, California, in the artillery unit. He wanted me to talk to someone else, another former Marine.

That fellow just happened to be working at the same screen company where I had a $1.25 an hour job. He said the Corps was tough when he'd gone through boot camp many years before.

"As a matter of fact," he said, "I got my butt kicked because I didn't do what the DI told me to do."

He started laughing. Then he asked me if I was going to the Corps. I told him I was thinking about it.

He said, "I know you. You'll probably make it okay."

So my brother and this guy both told me the same thing: the DIs will beat recruits who don't follow instructions, it's a tough branch, and if I wanted to join the Marine Corps, I'd better think twice. Once I got in, there'd be no turning back. Less than two years after signing up, I was a proud fighting Marine who'd been offered an incredible opportunity.

I kept daydreaming about wearing those shining gold bars on my collar. Then I'd remember all the young lieutenants we'd lost during the past few months. I didn't want to be one of those casualties. I figured my chances for survival as a lieutenant were fifty/fifty.

It sounded really good to go home with lieutenant bars, though. I didn't mention anything to the squad and gave the offer much thought. My mind was so conflicted. I was very young to be doing what they asked. I was already doing a lot for someone my age, for any of the men in Vietnam. But we were Marines. We had been trained well and we knew our duty.

The next day came without any incoming rounds for a change. The lieutenant and the gunnery sergeant showed up.

"Well," they asked, "what did you decide?"

"I'm honored, of course, sir, and pleased," I said. "Thank you for considering me for the promotion to lieutenant but I have to say no."

They were stunned.

The gunny said, "It's the chance of a lifetime. You should reconsider!"

"Is there a problem?" the lieutenant asked.

"No, sir," I said. "I have personal reasons for my decision. Plus, I don't think I'm smart enough to be an officer. And I really enjoy my duties as an NCO."

They both looked at me. "Are you sure?"

Even though my knees were still shaking, I told them I was sure. The whole time I wondered if I was making the right decision.

"Okay." The lieutenant turned around and walked out of the bunker.

I still had doubts but I felt relieved at the same time. Somewhere down the road, I knew I'd look back and wonder why I didn't accept the offer. If a phone had been available, I would have called my brother for his advice. He probably would have been happy to hear about me possibly being a second lieutenant. He always thought the Marine Corps was something special, and he would have known that only the elite could be leaders in that branch.

The subject never came up again and I tried to forget about it altogether.

* * *

The next day, I was summoned to the CP again. I thought maybe the CO was going to encourage me to accept the battlefield commission but when I arrived, a couple of Marines were standing outside the bunker. Maybe we were getting meritorious promotions to sergeant or receiving a medal.

A lieutenant ushered us inside to the Skipper, who was still tying his jungle boots. "A new Commandant of the Marine Corps (CMC) message came through," he said. "All personnel with two purple hearts must be removed from the combat area effective immediately. You're going back to the rear this afternoon."

"Will we still be in Golf Company?" I asked.

"More than likely you'll be assigned to the Third Marine Division Headquarters," he said.

My heart was glad but I also hated leaving all those new Marines and old friends behind. I knew what they would be facing for the rest of their own tours in country. I wouldn't be there to help them get through any of it.

Our truck would leave at 1400 hours. We were ordered to get our gear together. We all said, "Yes, sir," did an about-face, and marched out.

Well, we were a happy bunch of Marines. I shook each of their hands and wished them luck. Then I hurried to retrieve my gear. I gave my green book to the next senior Marine then walked around the fighting holes to say goodbye. They all wished me luck and told me they were happy for me. They were also sad because they wanted to leave with me.

"Who's going to look after us when you're gone?" they kept asking.

Finally I had to turn around and walk away. My feelings were so mixed I couldn't even look back. When I returned to the CP, the truck was already there. The engine was running but the driver was absent.

I looked around C-2 for the last time and remembered the very first day I arrived. I thought about the first taste of NVA artillery barrages and how we ran for the trenches like rabbits. I remembered how none of it had felt real. I also thought about the friends I lost in such a short time.

The driver reappeared and said I could sit up front.

He laughed and said, "Rank has its privileges."

I threw my pack onto the floor, which was dusty from all the red dirt. I tried to wipe some of the dust from the seat but it was useless. The driver told me he was going to move pretty fast in case the NVA spotters were out so I knew it would be a bumpy ride.

We waved at the Marines guarding the entrance. We went so fast that dirt, dust, and everything else in the road blew up behind us. The driver had no idea how fast we were going because his speedometer was broken. I just laughed as I bounced up and down with dust shooting out from under me every time I hit the seat. I really didn't care how fast we were going as long we got to Dong Ha in one piece.

We finally crossed the bridge near Cam Lo and hit the paved road on Highway 9. Then we made a straight shot to Dong Ha, passing small villages along the way. So far, so good; CH-46s were landing in the distance and I could almost taste the mess hall chow.

It didn't take long before we reached the gate. The driver drove up to the battalion headquarters and said, "Here you are."

I jumped down and struggled to get my pack over my shoulder. Even though the sun was going down, it was still hot out. I looked toward the DMZ and wondered what the men were doing and who was looking after them.

I finally checked in. One of the clerks said to come back the next day to get everything settled. In one of the company tents, my old cot, the one back in the corner, was vacant. I fished my mess kit from my pack and felt thankful I'd made it back in time for evening chow.

I was going to eat hearty in case this was my last evening meal in Dong Ha. I filled my canteen with hot coffee. I could tell it was strong because it was very dark. When I was done, I headed back to the company area to finish reading my mail. I had quite a few letters and wanted to get as much reading in as possible before night fell.

As I walked down the dirt street, I glanced at the DMZ and again thought about the men. I was very thankful to be in the rear and out of harm's way. Even though Dong Ha sometimes got rocketed, it was nothing compared to the front. Back in August, the NVA had blown up the fuel dump. The black smoke could be seen for miles. I hoped nothing that drastic happened that night.

I slept soundly for a change because I didn't have to pull watch. The morning came without incident. It was great watching the sun come up without being shelled or fired upon. The compound smelled of bacon, coffee, and all the breakfast foods. The aroma hit me as soon as I woke up. It sure smelled good, just like home cooking.

With breakfast out of the way, I stopped by the company office. The clerk told me to come back around 0800 when he would have my checkout sheet ready. I made sure my 782 gear wasn't too dirty then cleaned my weapon. I didn't want to turn in a dirty rifle to those armory guys.

By 0830 hours, I was ready. I was in good spirits, and the company office handed me my checkout sheet. If I could get done by noon, I might be able to catch the plane to Phu Bai that afternoon. I dashed off to turn in my 782 gear; next I went to the armory to turn in my weapon and extra ammo. At the battalion mailroom, I filled out my forwarding address form.

Everything was done just after 1000 hours. I rushed back to the company office. The clerk signed me out and gave me my orders. He told me my Service Record Book (SRB) would be forwarded through the mail.

At the airfield, the liaison said a CH-46 might leave for Phu Bai around noon. There was nothing to do but wait. The CH-46s were sitting on the pad. Finally we were told to board, and I ran out with the rest of the folks.

My job with Golf Company was done. I wouldn't be returning to combat. If I had taken the field promotion, I probably would have had to sign off on some papers to stay and fulfill that duty. But that was all in the past. I wouldn't see combat again. It seemed like it took forever for the CH-46 to lift off. I had my fingers crossed and said a little prayer as we rose into the air.

I thought about my time with Golf Company, where I'd started, where I'd been, what the company had done as a unit, about my lost friends, and about the friends I was leaving behind. Some of the men had been close to me; some were just acquaintances but all of them were my brothers. I wouldn't forget them as long as I lived.

I sat there mesmerized, still feeling like the whole thing was a dream and that I would be waking up pretty soon. I knew that some of the friends who'd lost limbs or suffered severe wounds would carry those reminders of the Vietnam War the rest of their lives. For those Marines, it definitely had not been a dream.

Epilogue

After leaving Golf Company, I checked in with the Third Marine Division, Headquarters Battalion, Headquarters Company in Phu Bai. About a month later, I ran into Golf Company's platoon sergeant one cloudy morning.

"I recommended you for a medal for your action on September 21, 1967," he said. "You deserve it. If you don't get it here, you'll probably receive it once you get back in the States."

I thanked him. Then we went our separate ways. That was the last time I saw him.

In April 1968, I was in Da Nang, South Vietnam for my flight home. There I ran into a Golf Company Navy corpsman on his way for R&R.

"I recommended you for a medal," he said, "for what you did during that firefight in September. Have you received it yet?"

I said no.

"Well, you should get one. You pulled out a lot of wounded Marines that day."

I thanked him. That was the last time I saw the Navy corpsman. I don't remember whether he mentioned the type of medal. At that point, I was just glad to be leaving in one piece. The recommendation must have been lost or misplaced during my transfer because it never showed up.

Now, so many years after Vietnam, I wonder about those medals and why I hadn't received them.

When I arrived home, my Mom gave me a big hug and hung on, crying the whole time. I patted her head, rubbed her back, and cried along with her. My sister who was pregnant with her first child was also there.

When I'd first walked toward the house, my Dad had gone into the kitchen. Just like when I'd come home for leave, he didn't want anyone to see him cry. After hugging folks in the living room, I went into the kitchen where my Dad and I hugged each other and cried. We wiped our eyes then rejoined the rest of the family.

Word got out I was home. Many people and relatives dropped by the house. There wasn't any ceremony but they did plan a dinner for me. Someone told me I should attend a powwow so the dancers could honor me as a veteran. But I'm not the type of person who would go just so someone could honor me.

My brothers who'd also served in the military didn't ask me about my experiences. Nor did I tell them anything. I knew they were proud of me and that was enough.

After completing my tour of Vietnam in 1968, I was assigned to the Fifth Marine Division at Camp Pendleton, California, as a management analyst. Less than a year later I was transferred to the First Marine Brigade in Hawaii.

When my service was up I re-enlisted for another tour, which eventually led to a career in the military. I retired with the rank of first sergeant after more than twenty-three years of honorable and faithful service.

In all that time, I never met up again with any of the Magnificent Seven from the original group I started out with in Vietnam. I've often wondered about them and if they made it back. I never met up with any of the survivors of the September 21 firefight either. I keep in touch with some of them by email and phone. There is a reunion of Second Marines, Fourth Battalion every summer but I've never attended. I hope to someday.

My wife, Maribeth, and I have been married since 1991. I have a daughter and a son from a previous marriage; my first wife has since passed away. I also have another son. All three of them have blessed me with eight wonderful grandchildren. They live in another part of the country so we spend more time talking on the phone than seeing each other in person.

I retired from a second career in 1997 and my wife recently retired. We moved several times in recent years for her career and made one final move to Texas after her retirement. I stay busy around the house with honey-dos and I dabble in art. My preference is a method called graphic art, which uses pen and ink and colored pencils. By stippling, I can shade certain areas for effect.

Despite all the difficult memories stirred up while writing this book, I did enjoy doing it. I may create another soon. Just like in Vietnam, I try to take things one day at a time. I really have a good life and enjoy it every day.

All these years later, I still vividly remember the wounded friends on the battlefields of September 21, 1967, and early on October 14, 1967. I often wonder if I'll ever see the survivors in person again.

It makes me proud to think of the extraordinary accomplishments of Golf Company, Second Battalion, Fourth Marine Regiment. I'll always have good memories of the men I consider friends. I'll never forget what we shared and accomplished as brothers–from the hills of Camp Evans to a little hilltop called Dong Ha and a place just outside Con Thien called Phu Oc.

We all had a job to do and we did it.

We were the best, second to none; we were "The Magnificent Bastards," a tribute bestowed on the Second Battalion, Fourth Marines on June 4, 1961 by then Commanding Officer Joseph R. (Bull) Fisher and made official by Commanding Officer A.E. (Gene) Bench on September 24, 1966.

Semper Fi

Made in the USA
San Bernardino, CA
05 December 2016